This book is a must-read if you are…

- keen to strengthen your leadership skills
- curious how women's rugby can inspire confidence in business
- ready to motivate and build high-performing teams
- seeking inspiration to lead a key project
- wanting easy-to-use self-improvement tools
- needing a pick-me-up
- eager to find a role model for you
- eager to be a role model for others
- recently retired from a career in sport
- curious about sporting intelligence
- needing to believe in yourself more

Praise for *The Captaincy*

"Women's sport is doing so well, due not only to female pioneers, but also to true male allies like Mark Francis; get ready to be inspired."
Gill Burns MBE
England Rugby Captain

"This book nails what Everest taught me – true leadership is guiding your team through a storm, not just reaching the summit."
Bonita Norris
Adventurer, climber, motivational speaker

"When I watch sport, I can tell who's winning without looking at the score. The Captaincy will show you how to do that too."
Professor Martine van Zandvoort
Clinical Neuropsychologist, Utrecht University

"Mark taught me a long time ago to be inspired by the thrill of success, not cowered by the fear of failure. Decades later, he's done it again."

Ramsay Jones CBE
Political strategist

"These are great insights into top-level leadership."

Gavin Hastings OBE
Scotland & British Lions Captain

"I'm still using what I learnt in terms of personal and collective mindset from Mark when we won a play-off final with Carlisle United at Wembley."

Owen Moxon
English Championship footballer

"Pick any leader's story in this book and you'll have yourself a ready-made success guide."

Becky Worley
Good Morning America and ABC News

THE
CAPTAINCY

*Leading Continues
Beyond the Game*

MARK FRANCIS

First published in Great Britain in 2025
by Book Brilliance Publishing
265A Fir Tree Road, Epsom, Surrey, KT17 3LF
United Kingdom
+44 (0)20 8641 5090
www.bookbrilliancepublishing.com
admin@bookbrilliancepublishing.com

© Copyright Mark Francis 2025

The moral right of Mark Francis to be identified as the author of this work has been asserted in accordance with the Copyright, Designs and Patents Acts 1988.

All rights reserved.
No part of this publication may be reproduced, stored in a retrieval system, or transmitted, in any form or by any means without the prior written permission of the publisher, nor be otherwise circulated in any form of binding or cover than that in which it is published and without similar condition being imposed on the subsequent purchaser.

A CIP catalogue record for this book
is available at the British Library.

ISBN 978-1-917534-10-9

For those who make themselves heard
when the world isn't ready to listen.

Contents

Foreword	1
Introduction	5
Chapter 1: Sporting Intelligence (SpQ)	9
Chapter 2: Why the World Needs More Female Leaders	27
Chapter 3: Paving the Path	47
Chapter 4: Change Makers of Tomorrow, Today	71
Chapter 5: What's Stopping You?	97
Chapter 6: Get Visible (Share the Good Stuff!)	117
Chapter 7: Gather Your Tribe	137
Chapter 8: Completer Mentality	155
Chapter 9: Making Connections	173
Chapter 10: Measuring Progress	191
Chapter 11: Taking Action	209
Conclusion	225
Further Reading and References	227
Glossary of Leadership Models	233
About the Author	237
The Role Model Effect: How To Be One and Find One	241

Foreword

It is now 27 years since I first encountered Mark Francis, who then was just a little way along the track which has made him such a brilliant influence on sportspeople and sports women in particular. I say *influence*, because the word 'coach' – conjuring as it does the image of some rasping bawler ranting on the touchline – is so ludicrously inadequate to describe the range of his talents, all of which are illustrated in this brave and significant book. We must now add the tag 'author'.

We spoke in Amsterdam in 1998 at the Women's Rugby World Cup, one of those bolt-on stuck-together marvels which paved the way for the modern-day World Cups. It paved the way for 42,000 joyous fans to attend the Stadium of Light when England kicked off the 2025 World Cup.

Mark told me back in 1998 that he was leaving the sport. I told him, *'You'll be back.'* Not every prediction I have made in *The Sunday Times* or to individuals came true, but he duly came back, with rugby sevens part of the sporting galaxy at his disposal. And as he illustrates in these pages, he has branched out to examine in depth so many inspirational individuals in business and in a glorious diversity of sports: ice hockey, basketball, rowing, tennis, golf and swimming.

Mark's reach is formidable. I love his concept of 'thin slicing' which I understand as improving the whole picture by prioritising one small aspect instead of trying to change a huge chunk – also his 'tribal fire,' or the inner power and passion which can be developed into individuals or team groups. In my experience, I have come across inferior teams who won because they wanted it more. More fire.

Mark's own underlying power comes partly from his experience of working alongside great female athletes and sportspeople; he suggests that they, his charges, were more significant than the lead he was giving them.

That may be too modest but he is correct to single many of them out – one of them is the great Gill Burns, the former England rugby captain who typifies his philosophy.

When I went to interview Burns in the nineties, I expected a tongue-tied young lady. She may be quiet but what a fine ambassador with a fanatical dedication to rugby (amateur, but total). Recently, I spoke to her again. She is the Queen of Rugby. Along with so many others, she proves the theory of Mark Francis that inspiration and improvement comes from a variety of sources, and definitely from both sexes.

We learn so much about some of the outstanding individuals who shaped Mark's own philosophy and powered their teams and/or sport – some of them well-known, others who deserve to be. We learn about the component parts of a team and their functions within the group. We learn from Sarina Wiegman, and a litany of other influential greats.

This book is a feast. It ranges across improvement philosophies in so many sports. It should become a textbook in its own right. It is accessible. It deserves attention.

Stephen Jones

Rugby Correspondent, *The Sunday Times*
Dorney, August 2025

Introduction

This book speaks to anyone who wants to lead something of value.

For the 40 years I coached elite women's rugby for club and country, I was never actually in charge. Instead, a remarkable group of pioneering women set the course, tone and standards for a fledgling sport in a male-led world. I followed their lead gleefully, whilst the external perception remained that, as the male coach, I must be running the show.

Many of the women who paved a path and paid their own way now lead in and beyond sport. This book is inspired by those and other Captains, who apply what sport taught them, to take responsibility for improving the wider community in which they live and work.

As a consultant, I travel all over the world collecting leadership stories. From 25 years of discovery, I have pinpointed eight distinctive traits of transformational leadership which I detail in this book. I'll also share the game-changing leadership models I have learnt, designed and delivered over the last four decades. Please steal them with pride.

More than a title or a position given to us for a specific task or team, *The Captaincy* is an ethos and a philosophy. It's an intention to change something that 'isn't right'. It's the boldness to lead even when there is no clear pathway or guaranteed support.

There are 60 Captain stories in this book. Fifty of those are about kick-ass entrepreneurial women. The stories create a **role model effect** to help you be one and find one. Discover a Captain here who inspires you and start modelling!

My favourite question to inspire a Captain is:

'What have you led that matters?'

Ask yourself the same question and make a note of your answer. In fact, I'd love you to start a Captain's notebook to capture your intent from now and as you read on.

My own answers to *'What have you led that matters?'* are:

The three consultancy businesses I have launched and led have made a difference in how:

- migration strategy is influenced by United Nations leaders at government level
- cardiac surgeons educate their heart teams and their own successors
- single mums in deprived inner-city areas find their first job

In each case, we establish and mentor internal change agents who own, lead and maintain the new approach. I call this 'Champion-led change' and 'Leader as educator'. It's the best way to ensure that valued changes are sustained.

When female athletes take charge, positive change happens. At its heart, this book is about:

- inspiring more women to lead
- sharing tips in leading positive change
- giving confidence to overcome self-doubt

Come on, let's find the champion in you!

Mark Francis

August 2025

Chapter 1

Sporting Intelligence (SpQ)

In addition to the known principles of IQ and EQ, great Captains also exhibit SpQ. This is the Sporting Quotient, an athletic intelligence which sets apart the greatest sportspeople. My invention of the term SpQ comes from my work as a player, coach, selector and ambassador within many sports. Applying the principles of SpQ will help you lead just as readily in commercial and not-for-profit sectors as it does in sport.

I see SpQ in all the best pioneering leaders in multiple fields. SpQ is a combination of Positive Intention, Self-Command, Thin-Slicing and Tribal Fire. See my design on the following page, showing how the four traits are interconnected.

At the heart of high performance is the ability to foresee great outcomes; to visualise success, to train your brain to expect it and your body to do whatever it takes to follow that script. It sounds simple because the body and mind act as one system; yet it takes relentless focus, self-discipline and a dedication to execute routinely well.

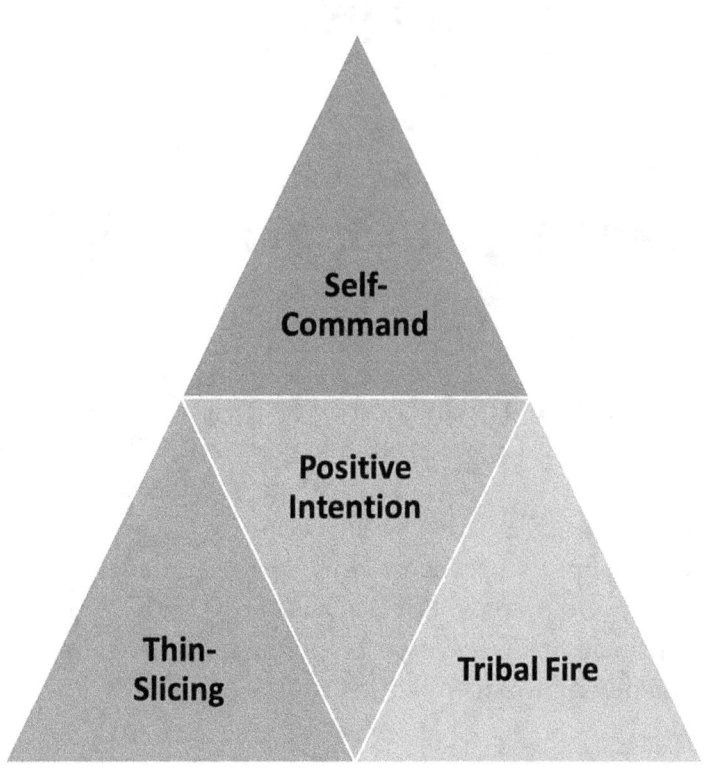

The best Captains create positive expectation and a collective intent. They lead by believing great outcomes are probable. They set a tone of commitment which lasts long after the mood in which that commitment was first made has disappeared.

At the UEFA Women's Euros in 2025, Sarina Wiegman coached the England team to victory by helping them win their last three knock-out games from a losing position, when in each game their opponents were dominating possession and territory.

Sarina Wiegman in Downing Street as a three-peat European Champion coach.

When she was asked, *'What makes this team so special?'* at the press conference straight after England's penalty shoot-out final win against Spain, Wiegman specified all four SpQ characteristics:

> 'It's about a real togetherness [tribal fire], tactical agility [thin-slicing], everyone's readiness to show up [self-command], and genuinely believing that you're going to win, no matter what happens [positive intention]'.

Positive Intention is the ability to visualise, manifest and reinforce the best possible outcomes and thus outweigh innate self-doubt.

When I work with professional football teams, I highlight the difference between 'playing to win' and 'playing to avoid losing'. Both mindsets are in their own way motivational, but when fear of losing takes over, it starts a negative spiral.

'Bazball-thinking' in the sport of cricket, for example, does not include options to play defensively or hang on for an honourable draw.

A combination of Coach Brendon 'Baz' McCullum and Captain Ben Stokes introduced a whole new way for the England Cricket team to approach Test matches, called 'Bazball'. This is a mentality which demands boldness, suspension of self-doubt and a forensic focus on positivity. It's a wholly new sporting intelligence in a highly tradition-led sport. Bazball has created observably more excitement for players and spectators and is helping to re-ignite interest in the five-day format of the game.

Since Stokes and McCullum took charge, attendances have grown by 25% for England matches, with the average age of spectators dropping significantly. Results have changed dramatically too, with England winning 13 of their first 18 Test matches under courageous Captain Stokes (having won just one of the previous 17 games). Importantly, there was only one draw in 18 matches, and that was only because it rained for two days in Manchester.

As an example of the importance of intention, AIK Stockholm Football Club were chasing the title in Sweden when I first worked with them as a mental coach in 2006. We knew if we won our last four matches, we would be the champions (as one of the remaining games was against the only team above us).

In the very next match, we scored a goal to take the lead with less than 10 minutes to go. The energy in our side changed palpably. Players looked tentative and nervous. We were demonstrably trying to protect the lead rather than aiming to increase it. The ball kept being played back to our goalkeeper rather than looking and playing forward. When the opponents equalised, it had felt inevitable. A disappointing 2-2 draw in that game meant AIK finished second in the championship that season; this was the result of a few short moments of negative mental framing and misplaced intent.

Thankfully, AIK had another chance to win the Allsvenskan in 2009 and they closed out the season as the number one team. The architect of the victory was Coach Mikael Stahre, a Captain I have since followed to varying degrees in Greece, China, India and the US leagues.

Self-Command is the ability to be composed and clinical when the pressure of the situation is at its highest, and when the self-doubt would normally be pervasive. That's when the strongest leaders, the Captains, stay in control of their own feelings and behaviours. They make smart choices whilst staying calm and in-the-present themselves. They execute actions resolutely and with full commitment.

A great example of self-command is my friend and client David Howell, a golf professional who was once ranked 9th in the world. David remembers the day he played a final round with Tiger Woods at the HSBC Champions event in China. David knew that his opponent was the best player in the world (and arguably the best golfer of all time) and would be breathing down his neck all day. At the same time, David acknowledged to himself that his own performances had been good enough during the first three rounds of the event to be leading the tournament deservedly:

> '*I kinda thought, **I am the number one right now**; I focused on hitting pure golf shots and smiling along the way. I didn't consciously think about what Tiger was doing at all, even though there was a huge, noisy crowd following our group and chanting Tiger's name. I played another good round and ended on top by three clear strokes as Champion!*'

David wasn't even the best golfer at his school when he was 15. Yet from that age, he told himself, '*I want to play golf professionally – it's way better than working for a living!*' He dedicated hours and hours to practice every day and got steadily better. Once a pro, David rose up the ranking each year without, as he terms it, '*getting in my own way overthinking outcomes before each competitive round.*' This is the essence of self-command. David has now played in 726 professional golf tournaments on the European tour, an all-time record.

I remember watching record-breaking American swimmer Katie Ledecky in the London Olympics when she was just 15. She raced like she was swimming for the fun of it; calm, smiling and completely unfazed by the occasion. Her coach Anthony Nesty commented recently: '*She trains like she's in last place, races like she's in first.*' Ledecky has SpQ at its highest level (humble, approachable and super talented) as these extraordinary stats show:

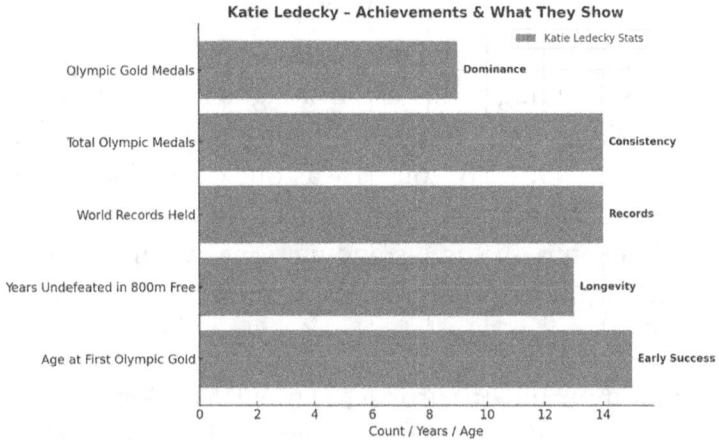

Thin-Slicing is the ability to make very quick inferences from minimal information and take smart, related action. In sport, it gives a two-second advantage over those who don't thin-slice (the majority). It's the opposite of overthinking.

The concept comes from Malcolm Gladwell's cracking book, *Blink*. It highlights the power of thinking fast and then acting instinctively. In its purest sense, it is when an athlete is so 'at one' with themselves and the situation, that they can express all their talent without checks or second thoughts. You may have heard the expression 'in the zone' or in the 'flow'. Mihaly Csikszentmihalyi's book, *Flow: The Psychology of Optimal Experience*, describes this simply as an individual *'feeling both energized and deeply focused in any situation.'*

In every deciding set Björn Borg played in five consecutive Wimbledon finals in the 1980s, he personified self-command and thin-slicing, aptly earning the nickname 'Ice Borg'. When he had just won his fifth title in a row, I bumped into him by chance at the top tier of the Centre Court stands. We both happened to be walking round the quietest corridor in the stadium. He was just soaking in his astonishing achievement and I was looking for a free seat, having watched the final in the standing-only zone. I was one of the many who had queued and camped overnight for the privilege of sprinting into the free-standing zone when the gates opened at noon. A Borg/McEnroe final made a sleepless night more than worth it.

In this moment of surprise, I asked Mr Borg eagerly what he did differently in 5th sets to be so invincible. He paused momentarily before saying, *'I focus even more on the ball – nothing else.'* This, I realise, is the thinnest slice a tennis player has when the gladiatorial battle rages.

Nat Sciver-Brunt is England Women's Cricket Captain and an archetypal thin-slicer. Described by her teammates as *'always calm'*, she is a clutch performer on the biggest stage scoring a half-century in a triumphant World Cup final in 2017 and the highest recorded century in a losing one.

I remember her in her schooldays at Epsom College where she was also a stand-out player in the boys first XI. In the shorter version of the game for England, she was trying to find creative ways to score faster runs and invented a shot, now known as the 'Natmeg', which uniquely sends the ball through her legs. Aptly, it's a thin slice!

Pattern recognition is an aspect of thin-slicing. It transforms split-second chaos into clarity, allowing athletes to anticipate plays, exploit weaknesses and proact with precision.

Tribal Fire is the ability to unify those around you with a shared passion for a common cause. It is also where there is enhanced strength derived from collective desire and an unshakable belief that can defy the odds, logical outcomes and all traditional expectation levels.

A great example of tribal fire is in my boyhood football club, Wimbledon, also known as 'The Dons'. Wimbledon has always been the smaller club by both size and reputation in every match they play.

In the 1980s, the self-dubbed 'Crazy Gang' of Dons players believed steadfastly that their fire-full, all-guns-blazing, collective spirit would always prevail (like David over Goliath). They got promoted to England's top league in 1986 (having been three divisions below that six years earlier) and won the FA Cup in 1988.

I paid a visit to the Hilton Hotel in Wembley on the evening before the final as I knew this was Wimbledon's overnight base for the game. When I arrived, the manager Bobby Gould was at the bar with his coaching team and I asked him how he felt the team would do. *'Oh, no worries, son, we're unstoppable.'*

I have worked as a mental coach for the more recent Wimbledon teams and I share with the new squads that story, emphasising the word 'unstoppable' delivered with unshakeable belief. It's an ideal mantra for a tribe in competitive sport, provided the whole team have bought in to the message with unwavering belief.

Leaders who generate tribal fire walk their talk and move in a common rhythm with their teams, as much in the hum-drum of day-to-day administrative tasks, as in key moments of performance delivery. In his pre-Test match team talk, former British and Irish Lions Rugby Union Captain, Paul O'Connell, demanded, *'Let's be the best at all the things that require no talent.'* It was a call to unify the tribe.

Tribal fire applies for an individual athlete too. Here's an elite list of solo sportspeople who spring to mind as creators of tribal fire: Steffi, Scottie, Sampras, Serena, Simone, Senna and Sinner.

Italian Jannik Sinner is the world's No. 1 male tennis player, doing it on his own with a detached coolness reminiscent of Björn Borg – and with a dedicated support team of two coaches, a physio, an osteopath and a PR manager. He has also inspired a fan base known as the Carrot boys (the 'Carota' in Italian); they are all helping to generate tribal fire, bolster their athlete during matches and inspire more followers.

Whilst the SpQ traits are often innate, they can be learned too. In his seminal work, *The Sports Gene*, David Epstein emphasises that athletic success often results from the right combination of genetic predispositions and environmental factors, including access to resources, training opportunities and mental resilience. In all the work I have done with professional athletes, the mental factors (SpQ) always determine the difference between the just very good and the truly great.

A great sportsman with high sporting intelligence is the former Scottish rugby player Gavin Hastings. In his heyday as Captain of Scotland and the British Lions, *The Independent* described his impact as *'Thundering without shouting'*. I love this description because it describes perfectly how Gavin inspired the tribe around him with a quiet inner confidence and thin-sliced communication. His actions 'thundered' louder than his words. Often, his greatest impact in a match was when the pressure was intense and the result was very much on the line.

In his 2021 book, *Legacy of the Lions*, Gavin emphasises that leadership is not innate; it can be learned and that great leaders are only great when the team around them is.

'Leadership', he says, *'like rugby, is a team effort. You win nothing on your own.'*

In the same mould, Karen Almond and Gill Burns, as the key leaders of England's World Cup-winning rugby team in 1994, generated tribal fire without the need to rabble-rouse their troops. They exhibited calm and humble leadership in all things off the field of play, then a calm authority with thin-slicing tactical impact on it. I loved watching them triumph at the Edinburgh World Cup in 1994 when I was with the Scotland team. Gill and Karen are amazing role models in the sport I love.

Try watching a sporting contest and measure (using SpQ) the competing coaches in terms of how they manage in-game decisions, like substitutions and tactical adjustment. In football, Carlo Ancelotti, Emma Hayes, José Mourinho and Pep Guardiola are stand-out examples of high SpQ in match-time decision-making.

Shaping Your Thoughts

How can you apply SpQ? **Cognitive reframing is a great start.**

Put simply, this means changing what you think and say to yourself in order to change how you do what you do. This is central to being a Captain. When you think and act positively, it changes your state, demeanour and body language. The mind and body operate as one system, so before trying to influence others, Captain your own thinking and mental state first. Reframing will often entail a chunk of self-reflection as to why internal thoughts are inherently self-limiting.

When England's talisman striker Chloe Kelly stepped up to take what could be the winning penalty against

Spain in the Euros final, she had already told her teammates, *'I'll score.'* If self-belief can be measured in the speed of a shot, then the 110 kilometres per hour of Kelly's strike speaks volumes.

Author Arianna Huffington's perspective on self-talk is poignant here:

> *'The greatest obstacle for me has been the voice in my head which I call my obnoxious roommate. I push back on it with a dose of wisdom.'*

Here's a powerful four-step model (which spells the word 'T.E.A.R.') for managing detrimental self-talk. Our <u>T</u>houghts lead to <u>E</u>motions, lead to <u>A</u>ctions, lead to <u>R</u>esults. To make the biggest difference to the end results, reframe your embedded (often unconscious) thoughts as a first step.

I learnt about T.E.A.R. from Kevin Walsh, a wonderful consultant and philanthropist from America, when we worked together in 2022. Watch out for his pending novel, *Leadership Lessons from Dogs Around the World*. A big thank you, Kevin, for the inspiration in this; you taught me that you can pronounce 'TEAR' two very different ways, as in *'tears of sorrow'* or as in to *'tear something up'* in a positive, go-getting way.

In his seminars, Kevin describes the model like this:

> *'If a situation is bad and you can change it… then change it! If it is something that you cannot change and is still a struggle for you, you can change the way that you view it.*

> *You get to choose how you go through it, either TEAR – Boohoo or TEAR – rip through; remember they're both a valid human reaction.'*

Have a think about a situation you are not comfortable with and which is causing some stress for you. What are the fundamental thoughts you have on the issue? When you think deeply about it, how does it make you feel?

Here are some examples of detrimental self-talk:

> *'I must try much harder.'*
>
> *'I'm getting old.'*
>
> *'I can't change the way I am.'*

Saying this to yourself will lead to self-deprecation, create anxiety, lead to action under stress and, ultimately, to underperformance.

Now take a look at the reframed self-talk example instead; it's personal, in the present tense and positive (the Three Ps of corrective self-talk):

> *'I live smarter every day.'*

Try saying that to yourself two or three times now. Does it make you feel more positive? Does it make you want to do something differently?

There are four elements to cognitive reframing to consider:

1. Avoid absolutes such as *'always'* and *'never'* – use less loaded words like *'can'* and *'do'* instead.

2. Change absolute, superlative language like *'worst'* or *'hardest'* – use words such as *'stretching'* or *'challenging'* instead.

3. Change from *'Why?'* to *'What?'* – replace *'Why does this always happen to me?'* with *'What can I do to ensure this does not happen again?'*

4. Exchange *'What ifs'* from *'What if I fail?'* to *'What if I learn and grow?'*

How about this reframe?

'I Captain real change.'

Changing just one or two words in your self-talk is conscious thin-slicing. As the great Serena Williams says:

*'Am I the greatest? I don't know. **I'm the greatest that I can be.**'*

There's more on the T.E.A.R. model in Chapter 4.

Your Leadership Intent

To help give context to the 'Captaincy' as a change leader intention, here's my working definition of leadership:

'Someone who guides us to a better place.'

It is about recognising what needs to change fundamentally and then determining to lead others in that new direction. It's absolutely **not** about positional power or hierarchy. It's about personal choice and a relentless intent to take action until the needed change has been realised and the Captain's job is done.

Think about your own current circumstances in their widest context:

- The business you work in
- The team you are part of
- The community you live in
- What makes you angry when you think about it?
- What one thing would you most like to change?
- What specifically makes you particularly furious?

Jot down the answers in your journal or notebook.

More than anything, I hope this book clarifies why the world needs more female leaders. It's written to inspire many more women to seek opportunities to Captain change in all aspects of life. It's written to help you be a role model and to find one.

At the end of each chapter, take a look at your notes and draw a table like the following one, then add the key insights you have gleaned from what you've read. The 'OH' column stands for *'Oh, I didn't know that about this before!'* Once you have written down all your OHs, decide what you intend to do as a result, starting with *'SO, I will…'*

Here are a couple of examples:

OH	SO
Thin-slicing will help me make faster, smarter decisions	Quit stalling on my must-do list
What matters and requires no talent?	Write a 'No talent needed' list for my key project

Are you ready to go on a journey that will transform the way you lead? OK, then, let's begin.

Multi-tasking Rochelle Martin won the Rugby World Cup with New Zealand three times. She is a Fire Department chief in Auckland, helped to raise $1 million for a children's charity and is a proud mum of four young children. Here's me toasting Roachy on a visit to Auckland near her family home.

Chapter 2

Why the World Needs More Female Leaders

The UN Secretary General, António Guterres, has repeatedly emphasised the importance of women in leadership, stating: *'Gender equality is a question of power, and power is still predominantly in the hands of men. We need to change that.'*[1]

The First World War showed a male-centric world what it had been missing in terms of female leadership deployment. With men away fighting, women entered the workforce in unprecedented numbers, taking on roles which had previously been deemed unsuitable. Aptitude for engineering, production, logistics, problem-solving and collaborative working was immediately apparent in the absence of men. The timing was perfect as this was the era of the Suffragettes in Britain, claiming simply that women should have an equal right to vote.

The Garrett/Fawcett sisters are role models who exemplify why we need more female leaders in this

---

[1] Women and Peace and Security Report of the Secretary-General, United Nation Security Council, S/2021/827, September 2021

world. Millicent and Elizabeth were raised in the late 1800s to believe that women were just as capable as men. Elizabeth went against tradition and advice to become the first female doctor and surgeon in England. In 1897, Millicent became President of the National Union of Women's Suffrage Societies.

Millicent's goal was to give women the right to vote. She recognised that this might take a long time and that it should ideally be achieved through discourse rather than more activist means. Her strategic influence, persistence and patience paid off when, at the end of the First World War, two of the most prominent politicians of the day changed their positions on gender capability entirely. In fact, Prime Minister David Lloyd George went from opposing suffrage to telling Fawcett at a parliamentary review meeting in March 1917,

> *'The women in war were wonderful. Their freshness of mind, their organizing skill, were magnificent. Men were making too great a mess of the world; they needed helpers without their own prejudices, idleness and self-indulgence.'*

I am sad that ego-driven men are still making a mess of the world in almost every aspect of nationhood, politics and organisational culture. Wanting to change that is a big reason behind writing this book.

As Home Secretary during the First World War, Winston Churchill's opinion was swayed too by observing at close-hand the game-changing impact that women had on the outcome of the war, especially when working in munitions factories, engineering and as decoders.

How do we build a fairer, more resilient world now?

My premise is that ensuring significant numbers of female leaders hold or share power in multiple sectors is essential.

We should aim for parity with the number of male and female leaders in society. Doubling the current number of female leaders would be a meaningful start. Women hold only about 28% of the managerial positions worldwide and yet make up over half the global population. Research from a McKinsey Pulse survey in 2023 shows that companies with more women in executive positions are likely to be 21% more profitable.[2] The survey doesn't simultaneously measure staff well-being alongside profitability, but if it did, ask yourself what it would show in terms of the quality of work environment and staff wellness.

In his brilliant podcast, *Re:Thinking*, Adam Grant shared that female-led states in the USA had markedly fewer fatalities from Covid than the male-led administrations.

The diverse governmental responses to the 2020 pandemic brought into stark contrast how female heads of state managed decision-making in a time of a global crisis. New Zealand's Jacinda Ardern's human style of messaging around every decision she made (and on a daily basis) was refreshing and symbolic. Her recently released book, *A Different Kind of Power*, is a must-read. One stat really stands out from the book. After the pandemic, Ardern asked a commission to assess how many lives had been saved by virtue of the leadership decisions her government had made. The conclusion is

---

[2] www.mckinsey.com/featured-insights/diversity-and-inclusion/diversity-matters-even-more-the-case-for-holistic-impact

that her conscious decision-making had saved the lives of 20,000 New Zealanders.

Stoic Angela Merkel in Germany also showed swift, clear and compassionate decision-making in the pandemic, and from my observation, that's how she led throughout her extended tenure as German Chancellor. The tone from both Ardern and Merkel was *'We're in this together,'* and *'We're with you all the way.'*

Call to Action

Which female leaders inspire you the most? Specifically, what is it about who they are and what they do that makes them stand out for you? What traits in them do you recognise in yourself, if any? Jot down your thoughts in your notebook.

In Britain, in stark contrast to Ardern and Merkel, the tone of party-boy Boris Johnson's daily press conference during Covid was *'Do it my way or you'll be punished.'* As the truth about his own behaviours during the pandemic surfaced, we saw he was a leader who repeatedly broke the strict rules he had set for the nation – one rule for certain people close to the decision-makers in power, and another rule for everyone else. People quickly fall out of love for the Captains who lead with ego, self-interest and the wrong set of values.

One clear example for me of the different impact female perspectives have on the big cultural challenges in society is the story of Trinidadian Claudia Jones. Born into working-class poverty and moving to an America rife with racial prejudice and segregation, she was imprisoned many times for her activism. She emigrated to Notting Hill in South West London in 1955.

Three years later, brutal riots took place in the area, fuelled by a build-up of racial tension. Claudia Jones founded a newspaper for the community, *The West Indian Gazette*, so her voice could be heard. Her proposed solution to violence was seen as radical by most in the government of the day.

Whilst the authorities wanted to respond to the riots with increased policing and tighter restrictions on nightlife, Jones was instrumental in promoting the idea of an annual carnival. Her suggestion was completely in the face of opposition from a male-led council, who thought a street party would be a trivial response to racist violence and that it would in fact increase the likelihood of unrest.

The annual Notting Hill Carnival still serves as Jones' legacy today. It is a symbol of multicultural unity, showcasing the power of community and cultural pride. Each year, around two million people gather in Notting Hill in a feast for the senses and in a celebration of humanity.

Il Mondo Diverso (The World is Richly Diverse!)

My core premise is that leadership-level decisions, such as Jones' Carnival solution to systemic rioting, are best made with a breadth of perspectives. In that sense, diversity of thinking, irrespective of gender, is needed. Carl Jung, the Swiss psychiatrist and psychoanalyst, (1875–1961) is the father of psychometric testing (personality profiling). He established that humans have four innate archetypes which shape our ideas and related behaviours. They are: the Self, the Shadow, the Anima/Animus and the Persona.

The Self represents unity and integration of the psyche. **The Shadow** is the darker, repressed aspects of one's personality. **The Anima/Animus** is the feminine side in men (Anima) and the masculine side in women (Animus). **The Persona** is the social mask we wear in public.

Given the 43 years I have coached in women's sport, I reckon I must exude ample anima!

Jung also introduced psychological types with two main attitudes: introversion and extroversion. The former is about drawing energy from within and the latter means being energised by external stimulants (such as a group of people to talk to). Importantly, Jung discovered that whilst there is no natural variance at all between male and female personalities, upbringing, societal norms and expectation has meant men exhibit more extroversion than women in group environments.

In practice, this means that in the four main character types, there is no gender propensity difference at all. The percentages of profiles in each personality preference are identical:

- red for task and results orientation
- blue for data and analytical energy
- yellow for ideas and possibility thinking
- green for principles and collaborative thinking

(The must-read book on this is *Surrounded by Idiots* by Thomas Erikson)

Take a look at the personality coded grid below. It will help you determine your natural preference as well as serve as a useful checklist for how to apply influencing skills on your Captain's journey. (It's my twist on the Colour Insights model.)

If you are a high yellow energy, positive intention and tribal fire will be quite natural. Alternatively, if you are a high blue energy, thin-slicing will be a hard behaviour to grasp! In my coaching experience, a combination of blue and red energy brings self-command innately, and green and yellow energy are essential for genuine, sustainable tribal fire.

Personality Energy	Verbal Style	Body Language	Top Tip
Tasky **Red**	Fast, Strong, Short	Clipped and Sharp	Be Direct and Short
Bubbly **Yellow**	Grins, Chatty, Bright	Big and Expansive	Match Energy
Calm **Blue**	Formal, Soft, Clear	Static and Smooth	Give Details
Peopley **Green**	Easy, Soft, Calm	Slow and Personable	Show You Care

Mike Brearley's cerebral book on leadership, *The Art of Captaincy*, emphasises how critical it is to adapt to the style of each person in your team: *'Captaincy is the art of working with people, not systems.'*

Whilst it is possible to have a group of thoroughly diverse thinkers all of the same gender, it is not possible to have diverseness of life experience and mentality without a gender mix. Fundamentally, that's why the world needs more female leaders; breadth of perspective, a collaborative instinct and a learned resilience from a lifetime experiencing a masculine prism.

In her thought-provoking book, *She's the Boss*, Noelle Ingram proposes reasons why the world needs more female leaders:

- Women are inclusive
- Women have more intuition
- Women tend to value work/life balance and emotions
- Women show empathy
- Women are good at multitasking
- Women defy the odds
- Women inspire more than they command
- Women don't speak for speaking's sake
- Women act as talent agents
- Women are more self-aware
- Women demonstrate emotional intelligence

- Women show resilience
- Women keep their ego in check

There are many multifaceted, multinational and multicultural female leader role models in this book. It's proof (if proof were needed) that your circumstances and upbringing should not/do not prohibit your ability and drive to lead.

In my rugby coaching, all the pioneering female leaders have brought three distinct traits:

- Level-headed, compassionate decision-making
- A drive to change what's not right
- A calm relentlessness

The need for role model leaders has never been greater; role models who lead with empathy are open to diverse perspectives, with a collaborative spirit. This is enabled by empowering more women to lead. In doing so, we can create more inclusive environments where more people flourish.

Missy Park's story brings these ideals to life wholeheartedly.

Missy Park

Missy Park was a friend long before she became a client. Her passion for basketball at high school in Greenville, South Carolina was passed on to her son Leo, who was destined for a professional sports career, until a chronic knee injury ended his dream. Missy played Division

The Captaincy

I love this photo of Missy Park in front of a wall of Change Captains.

One basketball at Yale University as well as lacrosse and tennis socially. Not that Missy plays *anything* without wanting desperately to win. Nowadays, as well as her Californian-based clothing business, Title Nine, she plays a mean game of pickleball, often in doubles with the equally competitive Jane Mitchell. Jane won the Rugby World Cup playing alongside her twin sister Emma with England in 1994.

Whilst her native love of competition fuelled Missy's love of basketball from a young age, she remained perpetually frustrated that the only sports clothes she could access were produced specifically for men. At Yale University in the early eighties, the women's team were given hand-me-downs from the men's squad and for some, it meant buying their shoes from the boys' section in superstores. At that time, there was no such thing as a sports bra, nor a female-focused sports apparel outlet anywhere in the US.

Missy gathered her teammates and declared:

> 'After graduation, we need to defeat the "shrink it and pink it brigade" and create a female equivalent of Nike ourselves.'

By 1989, 26-year-old Missy realised if this specialist business was to come to fruition, she needed to go it alone. She had saved up a relatively meagre $30,000 to produce a mail order catalogue exclusively for active females, or, as Missy calls them, in her rich southern accent, *'outdoorsy folk'*. Her intention was to create a direct-to-consumer business for people like her: aged over 20, active and outgoing in every sense.

She approached a number of clothing suppliers and asked for credit to be able to put their specialist female-targeted items into a 15,000-circulation catalogue. By chance, a sports bra company asked to be involved. They were an afterthought for Missy and only shown in the catalogue in black and white. Although she got just 15 orders from the first posting, each one of the orders included a sports bra. That one key insight helped to shape a business which has been going strong now for over 30 years.

Missy's business, Title Nine, was named after Title IX, the breakthrough legislation from 1972 that stated that all educational and sporting institutions in America had to give equal opportunity to participate for both sexes. Before 1972, just one in 27 women played organised sport after leaving education. The figure now is two in every five in America. For Missy, the positive impact of the Title IX legislation was that she could play a number of sports that her mother did not have the chance to do. Missy's mother was a trailblazer too, making most of the family's key financial decisions and negotiating 25% of a housemaid with her husband for every child they would have. Four children later, Mrs Park could delegate every menial household chore!

Title Nine made its first profit four very hard years after launch, mainly with the help of like-minded volunteers.

It gave Missy the chance to recruit Renee Thomas Jacobs, her first full-time employee. In 1995, they opened their first retail store. Remarkably, over 50% of customers came from at least two hours' drive away. It was evidence that Missy had created some committed and helpful tribal fire.

In 2000, Missy discovered the 'frog bra' sports bra which she was keen to sell. Crucial to that partnership with Renee was helping Missy's small team learn how to make their own version. In 2025, about half of what Title Nine sells is produced internally. The company has no debt and no external investors, and is a beacon for smart, values-based leadership. It is also, Missy hopes, a signal to would-be female entrepreneurs that anything and everything is possible.

> *'The key is to ensure that women have as many opportunities to lead as men do. It's an antidote to ignorance, just as founding your own business is an antidote to discrimination. It's our little place where we can build this business around women, owning and risking and leading in every aspect of the company.'*

Just think about that phrase: **'owning, risking and leading'**. That choice is open to all of us.

Missy is a transformational basketball coach at high-school level. She is technically sharp, innately competitive, super passionate and encouraging. She brings exactly that same energy to leading when she is in her Head Office. It means the team around her are fit for work, for play and for life.

Missy Park creating tribal fire for the Cougars.

When I asked Missy what she is most proud of, years after she founded Title Nine, she said:

> 'We grew this business from zero to $50 million not having one person who knew anything about retail, or apparel or business at all – just the pure passion about women and the transformative power of sport.'

Since 2016, Title Nine has sponsored a truly inspiring programme called Pitchfest, a twice-yearly opportunity for any female entrepreneur to present their products and business to a supportive local community in Northern California. The outcomes from the presentations vary from gaining direct investment, being given product placement in the 18 retail stores and digital catalogues, or being publicised on social media. All participants are given specific mentoring and coaching before their pitches (which is just like the BBC's *Dragons' Den* format, or the *Shark Tank* programme in the US).

You can have a great concept or product to sell, but if you can't capture attention and inspire listeners to want to buy, you'll be left disappointed.

I am blessed to be one of the two coaches provided to all the presenters at Pitchfest. My fellow coach, Becky Worley, is a TV journalist and broadcaster on *Good Morning America*. Becky and I run online sessions before the big day and help to do final prepping on the morning itself. Together, we help establish three main 'must apply' aspects to each pitch:

1. A.B.C.D. thinking, in this distinct sequence:
   - A stands for Audience
   - B stands for Behaviours
   - C stands for Content
   - D stands for Delivery
2. Start strongly, using a hook to grab attention
3. Authentic storytelling

A.B.C.D. thinking challenges our innate instincts about the order of presenting.

Our premise is that all preparation should begin by considering your Audience, **A**: What do they know? What do they need to know? How should you adapt to their style and expectations?

Next, focus on **B** for behaviours. What behaviours do you want to inspire in your audience both during your pitch and after you have finished?

With Audience **A** and Behaviours **B** in the front of your mind, you are ready to shape distinctly tailored content (**C**).

Lastly, you need to think about what style you want your content to be delivered in – **D** is for the Delivery method. It could be (as example options) facilitative, formal or story-based.

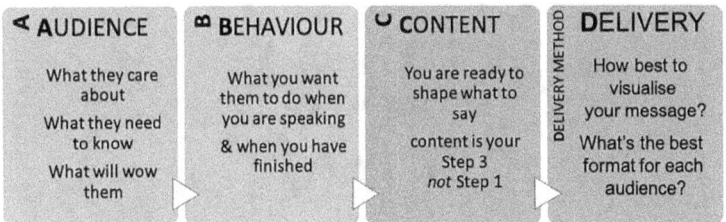

A AUDIENCE	B BEHAVIOUR	C CONTENT	D DELIVERY METHOD
What they care about What they need to know What will wow them	What you want them to do when you are speaking & when you have finished	You are ready to shape what to say content is your Step 3 *not* Step 1	How best to visualise your message? What's the best format for each audience?

The hook: We help all the Pitchfesters start their seven-minute speeches with impact. I created a simple visual to highlight the four best ways to hook an audience. Most business presentations I witness start like this: *'For those of you who don't know me, my name is...'*. Stop doing that! It's bland, uninspiring and deflating.

Aim to make every presentation you do start with one of the four ways to hook the audience:

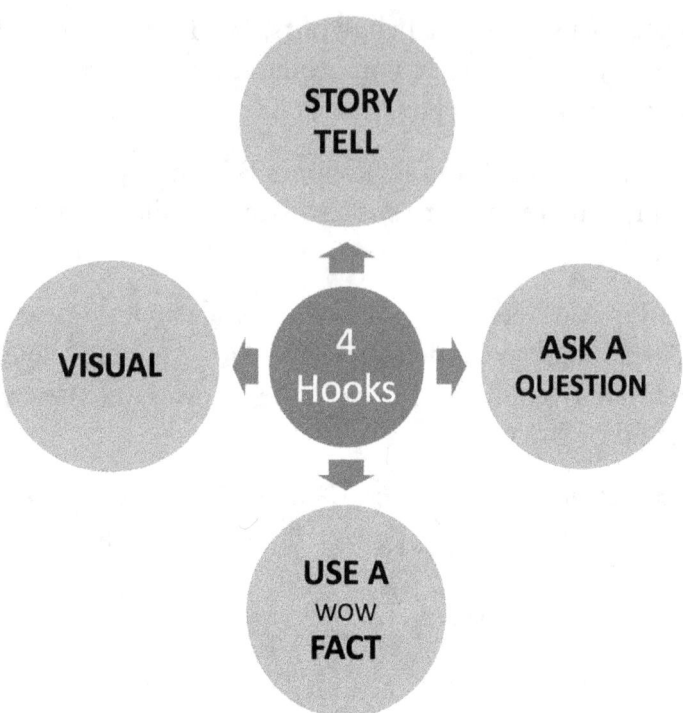

As I sat watching Pitchfest in the warm September sun in 2024, there were more than 100 inspiring, passionate and diverse women present from the 'tribe', including a grandmother, a young mum, two second-generation immigrants and a fresh-out-of-college business debutant. It tickles me that Missy calls all of them *'badass woman entrepreneurs'*! I was struck by the fact that what was in essence a competition with distinct winners also had an overwhelming vibe of genuine, palpable supportiveness. Our world needs loads more people with energy like that!

The trio: my fellow coach Becky Worley on the left (an all-American rugby player and Good Morning America correspondent), me and Pitchfester Robin Hall from Town Hall Outdoor Company, Steamboat Springs.

Missy sums up the pioneering spirit of 'badass' women entrepreneurs:

> 'The credit belongs to the woman who is actually in the arena, whose face is marred by dust and sweat and blood; who strives valiantly, who errs and comes up short again and again, because there is no effort without error or shortcoming.'

From my point of view, we need more female leaders like Missy because we need role models for future generations. Female leaders inspire young girls and women to pursue leadership roles, breaking societal stereotypes. This isn't simply about fairness either; it's about leveraging the full potential of humanity to create a sustainably better, more equitable world.

When women thrive, communities and economies thrive.

The Bottom Line

1. What are you passionate about that could do with a significant change? Does the concept/project have a clear and compelling Captain? Should it be you?
2. Be a badass entrepreneur; decide how much time and resources you will need to commit to have a distinctive and positive impact.

Call to Action

1. Thin-slice your thinking on how to achieve your goal.
2. Write a simple milestone plan.
3. Take the first step boldly.

Jot the answers down in your notebook.

Here's the chapter's reflective *Oh! And So?* to fill in or redraw.

OH	SO

In the next chapter, you'll meet some groundbreaking women who paved the path for others to follow. These pioneers let me be their sports coach, so I had privileged access to a woman's world full of Captains. The insights shared from their stories will help to inspire the Captain in you.

Chapter 3

Paving the Path

Think of a time when you decided to try something new, different and meaningful for the first time. Something that required a bold decision to get going and a good deal of effort and leadership on your part.

It might have been a charitable initiative, a help group of some kind or a new business entity. It may have seemed insignificant at first. Now reflect on who was inspired by your initiative. How many people did it impact? Give yourself a pat on the back! No matter how big or small this initiative was, you were paving a path.

Paving a new path doesn't always mean creating something entirely new. It can mean redefining the ordinary by flipping the lens and seeing what others have missed. It's less about innovation and more about rebellion. The stories in this chapter are about people who are rebels with a cause. They have set an example which others can follow.

Emily Campbell

When Emily Campbell won Great Britain's first ever Olympic weightlifting medal at the 2021 event in Japan, it was her vibrant personality and flair which caught people's imagination. Inspired by her demeanour as much as her silver medal, I started following her on social media. When she's in competition, Emily switches on her high sporting intelligence quotient.

She has won five consecutive European Championships which has helped to magnify her persona and inspire more girls to see weightlifting as an option for a healthier life.

She has used this platform to be a Captain in her community near the city of Nottingham and is an advocate for body-positive messaging. She is planning to open a gym near her hometown as the base for encouraging more girls to be active. She wants to leave a legacy far beyond her weightlifting. It's a legacy which empowers girls, enables more community connection and champions inclusivity.

Leaving Footprints

Two major sporting events concluded on the last weekend of September 2025. In both cases, the winners highlighted just how important the exploits of their successful predecessors had been in laying a path to follow for the current era of players.

One spectacle was the biannual Ryder Cup tournament in golf, which saw Europe retain the trophy 15-13 on a dramatic final day against a powerful American team, who were playing on home soil.

European Captain Luke Donald called out the successes of the past in helping grow levels of positive intent within his current team of 12:

> 'We drew strength and inspiration from the 37 European players who have won this Cup away from home before. This week, we were determined to add 10 more.'

The other major sporting event that weekend was the Women's Rugby World Cup final, with England winning the trophy for the third time, defeating Canada at Twickenham. Triumphant England Captain Zoe Aldcroft remarked on the importance of legacy too:

> 'We have been on a journey "for the girls". It wasn't just about the girls in the circle now; it was also the girls we inspire to follow us, and to honour the girls who have come before us.'

Emma Mitchell, World Cup winner with England in 1994 with the World Cup won by the current England team in 2025.

This sentiment was backed up when all past winners of the World Cup were invited to the England post-match celebrations on 26th September.

There were four key people who were instrumental in paving a path for England's recent victory.

Mary Forsyth, Sue Dorrington, Alice Cooper and Deborah Griffin

In 1987 when rugby was still an amateur sport, the International Rugby Football Board (IRFB) hosted its first Men's World Cup in New Zealand. Two years later, the Richmond Women's team toured New Zealand wholly self-funded. They played nine matches against the best club teams in the land and the powerful regional sides from Auckland and Canterbury. Uniquely, the club won nine out of nine touring matches. Our senior players decided on that tour that the women's game needed more international competition to truly make the sport thrive.

Four Richmond players believed there should be a Women's World Cup in Britain in 1991, to coincide with the men's tournament. Mary Forsyth, Sue Dorrington, Alice Cooper and Deborah Griffin presented a proposal to the Women's Rugby Football Union suggesting they should host a global tournament. Once sanctioned, the four pioneers devised, communicated, influenced, organised and partly self-financed a groundbreaking tournament. This was done despite a mixture of lethargy and active opposition from the sport's male-dominated governing body.

In addition to managing the finances, they set up the schedule, logistics, communication, transport, accommodation, pitches, officials and press coverage.

Debs Griffin, Sue Dorrington, Alice Cooper and Mary Forsyth, all in the Rugby Hall of Fame, are pictured in the Richmond Trophy Room.

The tournament boasted 12 teams, including Japan, Canada, Russia, France and the USA.

The glorious book *World in Their Hands* by Martyn Thomas delves into the extraordinary challenges faced in making the first Women's World Cup happen; ingrained misogyny, economic recession, the Gulf War, the collapse of the Soviet Union and a lack of eager – in fact, any – sponsors in women's rugby.

As well as playing rugby at Richmond, all four women had their own business careers to manage and two of them, Debs and Mary, also had young children to nurture.

It is fitting that the launch of *The Captaincy* in 2025 will coincide with Deborah Griffin OBE becoming the first woman to become President of the Rugby Football Union in England. The RFU is one of those traditional

British institutions which is notoriously rooted in conservative judgement and stubborn masculinity.

In 1995, the then England men's Captain, Will Carling, described the decision-making at committee and organisation level as being *'run by 57 old farts'*[3]. *'Male, pale and stale'* was his associated reference. To reinforce the very point he had just made, those *'old farts'* instantly sacked him as Captain. Even though a public outcry saw him reinstated, the principle of governing bodies requiring younger, smarter leadership had been well made.

One decision made by female sports leaders following that first Women's World Cup was to no longer arrange the tournament in the same year as the men's event. Doing so made it much harder both to organise the women's tournament and to garner significant media interest and sponsorship.

Whilst the sport's governing body, the International Rugby Football Board (IRFB), initially sanctioned the second World Cup – this time in Amsterdam, due for April 1994 – they had a change of heart just 90 days before the first game was due to take place. They cancelled the whole tournament without a clearly stated reason. The clearest example of dismissive sexism I have experienced in 60 years on this planet! Can you imagine what that felt like for athletes who had already booked time off work and paid their way to represent their countries?

---

[3] https://www.therugbyjournal.com/rugby-blog/will-carling

The IRFB did more than just cancel the 1994 event; they threatened the Dutch RFU (men and women) with permanent expulsion from the Union. The male-dominated international board stated that the 1991 and 1994 events could not be called World Cups as they had not been sanctioned by them. It took until 2008 for the female-run tournaments to be officially recognised. It's just pompous, masculine nonsense.

Sue Brodie and Sandra Colamartino

Sue Brodie, an international player and the chair of the newly formed Scottish Women's Rugby Union (1993), decided that Scotland would step in bravely to host the 1994 event. With just a year's administrative experience, Sue and her committee gathered like-minded players and willing volunteers to set the project in motion.

Sixty days before the due start, Sue sent invitations to all countries with a national team to be in Edinburgh for the World Championship on the same dates which had been planned for Amsterdam.

Then, in a spiteful move, the IRB refused to sanction Scotland's bid! Sue, therefore, had no formal approval, no funds and initially no teams. Many had been forced to withdraw by their male-led unions, unable to rebel against the governing body. Much like the pioneers of the first World Championship, Sue refused to be defeated and when a handful of teams confirmed attendance, more followed. The tournament took place as planned, on time, with 12 competitive teams and with significant media coverage.

Kim Millar, playwright who was instrumental in making '90 Days' such a memorable musical play.

This remarkable achievement has inspired a musical stage play called *90 Days*, inspired by Sandra and written by Kim Millar[4], in which Sue and the Scottish team's first captain, Sandra Colamartino, are depicted embracing a seemingly impossible idea: hosting a global event from scratch with just three months' notice.

Opening night of '90 Days'.
Bottom row: Dani Heron (who played Sue Brodie) and Yana Harris (who played Kim Littlejohn, Scotland's World Cup Captain, succeeding Sandra).
Middle row: the real Sue and Kim.
Top row: two current Scotland internationals.

[4] https://www.traverse.co.uk/whats-on/event/90-days-spring-24

90 Days premièred at the Traverse Theatre in Edinburgh, 30 years to the month after the 1994 World Cup in Edinburgh. Apart from her athletic prowess as Scotland's first ever Captain, Sandra Colamartino has been a leading magazine editor and runs her own confectionery business, Quirky Chocolate. I'll share more of that sweet story in Chapter 8.

Perhaps most remarkable of all in these two stories of administrative prowess on a global scale, is that the captaincy of change in each case had no detrimental impact on the playing performances of those involved. Richmond were crowned National Champions in 1990 and 1991; Sue Dorrington played with England in 1991 and made the final; and Sue Brodie played in the winning Plate Final in 1994 that saw a newly-formed Scotland beat strong favourites Canada for fifth place overall.

Sister Davi

The most extraordinary path-paver I have met is Nora Allen Stenger, who started her working life as a farm girl. When she was 12, she was in a tractor, working solo, when it broke down. With no other option, she found a way to fix it herself, by trial and error, plunging all 5 foot 2 inches of herself deep into the engine! Nora's time on the farm turned out to be a great foundation for the challenges she was to face as a soon-to-be distance-travelling nun.

I met Nora at a leadership congress in Sao Paulo in 2016. She was a guest speaker talking about how to galvanise a community to help itself to grow and prosper. She recounted how even at the age of 80, she was still an active member of the Teresina community in North Eastern Brazil, cajoling its citizens to give up time to make life better for all. I promised that if she would let me interview her about leadership traits, I would give her one of the conference T-shirts with the words 'Live your best self' emblazoned on the back. The photo below is of Sister Davi (her Brazilian name) wearing that T-shirt. *'It makes me look hip!'* she said with a grin.

86-year-old Nora Stenger (Sister Davi) at breakfast in Sao Paolo, feeling 'hip'.

When Sister Davi first arrived in the rainforests of northern Brazil on a Papal mission in early 1963, nothing could have prepared her for the primitive environment into which she was thrown. The community of Teresina had no electricity, no running water and no healthcare facilities. Sister Davi decided that a multitude of basic infrastructures had to be built as a priority. She already knew there would be no funding or help from the government, which was why the Papal mission had been sent there in the first place.

When she discussed the need to build a hospital with the local community, she saw a surprising degree of lethargy from the male-led council. She knew how to sort that.

I asked her a question worthy of all great leaders.

'What Superpower did you use?'

She replied with a wry smile:

> 'Oh, that's easy: self-reliant problem-solver! Get the world to follow you by just getting on with it yourself. Don't hesitate to get stuck in and show a "just do it" energy. I grew up with brothers on a farm in Kentucky and my problem-solving, competitiveness and self-reliance stems from that.'

She continued,

> 'When the hospital needed building and the local men were plain lazy, I shamed them into doing the work by building the entrance wall myself. When I had appendicitis 10 years later and I discovered as a patient that our beds had cockroaches, I didn't wait for the local government to find a budget for replacement beds. I burnt all the hospital beds in a huge fire outside the Mayor's house. We got our new beds really quickly after that...!'

Sister Davi was a rebel with a cause.

The facilities in Teresina today are something Sister Davi is very proud of: there is the largest emergency hospital in the region, a small airport, a highly-rated university, multilingual schools and a pretty decent Wi-Fi signal. Sister Davi had an active hand in all of these projects.

'*I don't really do social media,*' she told me, '*but I can blog and vlog if I need to get a decision-maker to stop faffing about!*' Sister Davi had a Captain's mindset for sure – leading by example and being relentless with it. The infrastructure in the now-thriving community of Teresina is a great legacy to Captain Davi. At our breakfast, she had two plates of food and two coffees. '*I don't usually have food made for me, so I'm optimising while I get the chance!*' I smile every time I think of her.

How do you trigger a drive to lead something substantial like Sister Davi's mammoth infrastructure project? There are three sequential steps which will help to do just that: introspection, visioning and road-mapping.

Step One: Introspection

This is a thorough analysis of who you are and who you want to be. What is your essence? What are your core values? How can those be best served by dedicating to one particular cause?

Blaire Palmer

Blaire Palmer is a former BBC producer, consultant and bestselling author. Seek out her latest book, *Punks in Suits*. It's all about Captaincy in the business world. It's brilliant and inspirational.

In the early 2020s, Blaire went through the trauma of witnessing her mum suffer and die from dementia. Conscious that she was entering her fifties soon, Blaire felt that perhaps her fate was inevitably going to result in a similarly painful, physical and mental decline.

One day, soon after her mum passed, Blaire looked at a photo of herself. She was unimpressed and distinctly dissatisfied by what she saw. She made an instant decision to change both her physical and mental state. She reflected that self-talk was just that: talk! It wasn't and needn't be her reality. As a result, she was determined to take control of her own destiny and immediately hired a personal trainer.

Blaire Palmer posting on her popular social media channels.

Within a few discipline-filled, diet-smart, gym-embracing months, she became a bodybuilder and gained her own personal trainer qualification. I see her in sleeveless outfits whenever we meet and it's a signal that she is rightfully proud of her toned body.

I love meeting up with Blaire when we can because she embodies mindfulness and positive introspection. Time with her makes me want to bring more discipline into my daily routines. She paved the path for me to get back into an exercise routine to reshape the next phase of my life.

Step Two: Vision

To embrace a vision of a better place, every great leader I've met or studied has a drive towards something demonstrably better, usually much, much better than the current situation. Having a vision compelled them to reach the better place, no matter what sacrifices were needed on the way.

When I was coaching the fledgling Scottish Women's rugby team in 1993 (our first competitive year), we set a clear vision, which was:

> *'To be cheered by the crowd wherever we play, because of the way we play.'*

We felt that this philosophy and mentality would help grow the fan base for the sport, as well as to condition our young squad that just winning wasn't really what should drive us. We should focus more on our role as pioneers of a still fledgling sport – if we played exciting, cheerful rugby, more girls would want to take up playing too.

Within three years, we were playing in the European Championship semi-final in France against Spain. We hung on enough to win in a nail-bitingly tight match. Exhausted and relieved, the squad jogged towards the tunnel and the whole crowd in the main stand stood up, cheered and chanted, *'Scotland! Scotland!'*, clapping in rhythm with the words. As the vast majority of the crowd were not Scottish, this was a lovely, spine-chilling recognition that our dream was coming true!

Our mission (the tangible part of the bigger vision) in 1993 was for *'paying spectators of women's rugby.'*

At the time, this was a pipe dream, given that the people paying were the players themselves and, in most cases, the crowd contained family members, partners, family pets and the coaching staff. Yet, 30 years later:

- More than 18,000 spectators paid to watch Harlequins play Leicester in a women's club game.
- In 2023, 58,000 people paid to watch the England versus France title-deciding match.
- In 2024, 80,000 attended every session of the women's sevens competition at the Paris Olympics.

Your Turn

The following exercise should help you create **your** vision. Ideally, ask someone to be your guide as this works best when you allow your conscious brain to switch off and your deeper consciousness to come alive. You can self-coach too and that's where NLP (neuro-linguistic programming) can help.

Dr Robert Dilts is a psychologist renowned for modelling excellence within the theory of NLP, which, put simply, is brain-language flexing. It enables self-coaching, especially when you allow your subconscious brain to play a role. His 'logical levels' pyramid shows six levels of change, with my added questions.

On the following diagram, start at the bottom with the environment. Then work your way up the pyramid to your mission, to gain clarity and insight.

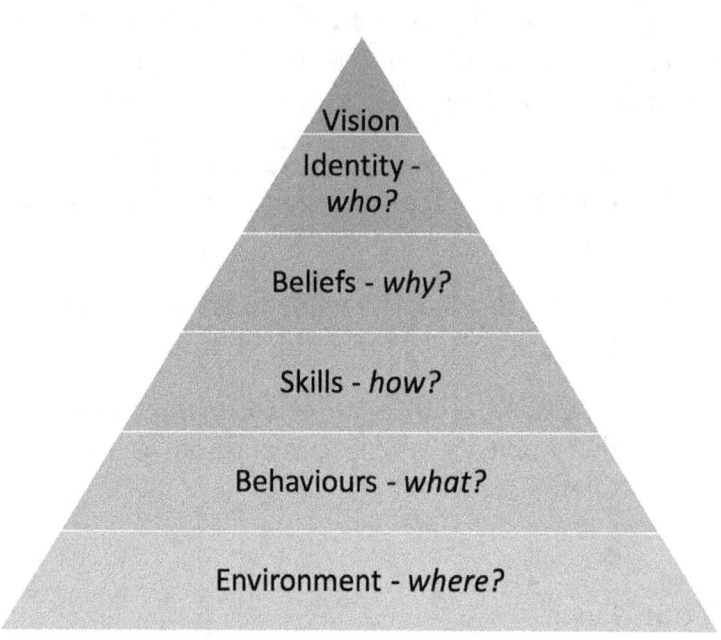

Self-Guided Coaching To Crystalise Your Vision

Start by sitting in a chair in a quiet place (ideally a noiseless room with no distractions). Make sure you are comfortable and that your back is fully supported. Sit up straight with your feet firmly on the floor, shoulder-width apart.

Decide your goal intention. Is it to do with your next career move? Is it about the team you are in or lead? Is it about the place you want to live in or move to? Keep whatever you choose as your focused intention in the front of your mind.

Focus on your breathing alone. Listen to your breathing and feel your breath going gently in and out. Sense how calming it is.

Concentrate on breathing in through your nose and breathing out through your mouth. Reflect each time that you are breathing *in relaxation* and breathing *out any tension or anxieties*. As your body is relaxing, your mind remains as sharp as a pin.

Imagine a moment in the future, perhaps a year or two from now.

Place yourself in the new experience fully.

- **Environment:** Where am I? What can I see? What is happening around me? What sounds can I hear? How does it make me feel?

- **Behaviours:** What am I doing in this situation? What specific actions am I taking? How am I behaving in this environment?

- **Skills:** What skills and specialist knowledge do I have? How am I using my skills to achieve my goals? What strategies or resources do I use?

- **Values/Beliefs:** Why am I doing this? What do I believe about myself whilst doing this? What is most important to me in this situation? What do I value in this context?

- **Identity:** Who am I in this situation? What kind of person am I when I do this? How do I see myself in relation to this experience? What role do I play?

- **Mission:** What is my larger purpose in this? What am I ultimately serving or contributing to? What is the bigger picture or meaning behind it? How does it align with something larger than myself?

Make a note of your answers in your notebook or journal.

When I did this exercise, Chin-Ning Chu (more on her later!) asked me these questions as a mentor and a benevolent protagonist. Consider who could best fulfil the coach's role for you.

Step Three: Road-Mapping

The third key step in triggering a Captain mindset is all about taking purposeful, resilient action – road-mapping that journey and starting quickly. You have a clear and compelling vision of where to go and the key components required for it. Next up is to create a workable plan that both sets the path and enables a clear, smart and fast first move.

In the fledgling Scottish Women's rugby team in 1993, we knew we needed more strength and depth in our squad. The target was to have two credible international-standard players in each playing position. Our clear, smart, and fast first move was to form a Scotland second team, known in rugby as the Scotland 'A' team. This gave a whole new set of aspiring players a platform from which to develop and shine.

There are two proven ways to set a route-map plan. Choose the one which best suits your colour energies (see Chapter 2), your character, and the key change you wish to initiate. One way is to plan with the end in mind first.

Option 1: Backward Planning

This method begins with the end goal in mind, planning backwards.

With the Scottish team, our core goal in 1993 was to be European Champions by 1998. Working backwards from there, we worked out what needed to happen in 1997, 1996, 1995 and 1994 in order for us to ensure we'd reach the higher goal.

Here are our backward planning headlines set in 1993:

- 1998: Play direct and smart and be the number one women's team in Europe (remaining undefeated).

- 1997: Train with Olympians at a winter camp in Club La Santa with the full squad.

- 1996: Have measurably the fittest squad in Europe.

- 1995: Use music to bind all and establish a winning mentality (arrange winnable fixtures only this season).

- 1994: Find key sponsors and reach the quarter-finals of the World Cup in Amsterdam, with two credible players in every position in the team.

Option 2: Milestone Planning

This method creates a high-level plan which follows a sequential logic and chunks up lots of activities into key stepping stones. It is project management theory in practice.

Here are the milestones the 21-year-old sports entrepreneur Arun Watkins set himself for his EggChaser Rugby Sevens Academy when it was launched in 2023. Arun's business focuses on providing multiple opportunities for young athletes to play rugby. He also has a sports clothing business and a retail store in Reigate, Surrey.

1. When the first rugby club signs a kit-supply partnership with EggChaser.

2. When we have full-time Academy coaching staff in all counties in Britain (with partnerships in local schools and rugby clubs).

3. When EggChaser hosts its own competition, with a minimum of 150 playing participants under the age of 18.

4. When the first Academy-developed player receives their first full international cap.

Notice how the milestones are stepping stones towards a higher goal? The first milestone is about a financial platform and local networking. The second milestone is about geographical expansion, to reach many more players. The third milestone is recognition that the breadth of coaching has produced a good quantity of committed athletes. Only milestone four is yet to be achieved by Captain Watkins. That hasn't stopped his playing teams, known as the Lions and Lionesses, from scooping up trophies in America, Africa, Europe and at the prestigious Dubai Sevens International (there's more on Arun's story in the next chapter).

Anika Tiplady: A Parent, an Athlete and a Leader in Business and in Her Community

When we met in 2005, Anika Tiplady didn't think she could have it all. She was a Captain in the New Zealand Army at the time and had just played a rugby match for the Army XV against the Richmond team I was coaching. As you will see, there are in fact multiple aspects of Anika's life in which she triumphs.

After the game against Richmond in which she stood out as a player and a leader, I asked Anika if she would consider playing for our team at Richmond and perhaps using that as a springboard to become a full New Zealand international. At first, she was sceptical that she even had the ability to be a full international. New Zealand's women were ranked No. 2 in the world, behind recent world champions, England. How could she maintain an Army career and dedicate enough time to be an elite athlete as well?

Our conversation clearly triggered Anika to aim high and to set complementary life, career and sporting goals. She took a year's sabbatical from the Army to play a season for Richmond Rugby Club. It led to an international call-up. With three caps under her belt, she took time out of rugby to dedicate solely to her military career. You'll notice a trend of dedication to one key element at a time. When was the last time you took a sabbatical?

When she retired from rugby, Anika took up two new passions: football and a career in medicine. She won the national title in soccer with her team, Mainland Pride, and simultaneously graduated from the University of Otago Medical School in 2016.

Dr Anika Tiplady, inspiring as a player, captain, coach and team doctor.

The honour roll for Dr Anika Tiplady is rather impressive. She first represented the full New Zealand rugby team in October 2007. As a soldier, after serving tours in Syria and Lebanon, she was awarded the United Nations Outstanding Contribution Medal. In 2012, the Otago Rugby Union declared it had no funds to support the women's team. Anika, as the then team Captain, led the fundraising which delivered the $20,000 necessary for the team's whole season. She is now team doctor for the New Zealand national football team and the men's Canterbury region rugby team. She is also a present and dedicated mother to her young family.

Jot down some reflections on what areas of passion and intrigue would spark your interest in paving and leading a new path.

The Bottom Line

1. Choose a path yet to be walked. What do you want to be a pioneer in?

2. Set a compelling vision and main milestones – the stepping stones along the path.

3. Start boldly and resiliently so that your energy and demeanour can inspire followship.

Here's this chapter's reflective *Oh! And So?*

OH	SO

In the next chapter, *Change Makers of Tomorrow, Today*, you'll meet some groundbreaking young entrepreneurs for whom age has had no restraining impact either on their desire to be Captains, or on their immediate impact in the aspirational, self-assigned roles they've embraced.

Chapter 4

Change Makers of Tomorrow, Today

The best days are the ones of eyes wide open with surprise or euphoria. The moments when your paradigm of what is right or wrong, new or just special, gets challenged or wholeheartedly reinforced by a new observation or experience. One such day for me was when I shared the stage at a Paradigm Shift Conference in 2024 with Sally Spicer. The topic was 'Mastering multigenerational leadership'. Sally, an expert in recruiting, leading and developing talent, opened her talk with this statement:

> 'Gen Z[5] contains the largest numbers of any generation in the world today. It's the wealthiest generation and is, by some margin, the most generous.'

The audience took a deep intake of breath, looking surprised by Sally's opening. They were hooked.

---

[5] Generation Z is classed as those born between 1997 and 2012.

In this chapter, I show how to optimise the values and drive of the younger generations and how to gear yourself up to be a change-maker yourself. The examples I share are mainly younger trailblazers from Gen Z or young millennials. These are the new Captains you'll need to influence, compete with and inspire.

There is a prevalent myth that Gen Z is demanding, entitled and difficult to manage. However, detailed research from Lucy Kemp reveals a much more nuanced picture. See her paper *'Understanding and empowering gen Z in the workforce'*.[6] Unlike the 'lazy' or 'entitled' stereotypes, Gen Z is a generation shaped by socio-political upheavals such as the 2008 financial crisis, the rise of social movements like Black Lives Matter, the #MeToo movement and the Covid-19 pandemic. These events have cultivated a pragmatic, resilient mindset within this cohort, characterised by a need for authenticity, transparency and stability. They are all about a life of F.I.R.E. – Fast Impact, Retire Early! As you will see, that means these under-thirties are often focused and driven and will not (as older generations do) suffer managers or businesses with a top-down, controlling culture.

Lucy Kemp's research aimed to understand the workplace needs, aspirations and challenges of Gen Z, focusing on gender differences and the evolving role of Gen Z women. Lucy's analysis used a multimethod research approach, which included a comprehensive survey of over 2,600 Gen Z members, in-depth focus

---

[6] https://static1.squarespace.com/static/65bd14faf47a332d026d9d3e/t/66 1cdeb08458e4407e81ea88/1713168084089/THE+GEN+Z+BLUEPRINT+ Building+a+Workforce+that+Thrives+on+Innovation+and+Inclusion+15 0424.pdf

group discussions and one-on-one interviews. Seventy people managers were also interviewed to gain insight into their experiences working with Gen Z employees.

Gen Z is often wrongly characterised as 'digital natives,' a label that oversimplifies their identity. While technology is an intrinsic part of their lives, Gen Z values human connection, meaningful impact and psychological safety in their workplaces. Gen Z men and women both demonstrate a desire for work/life harmony, although the factors driving this vary. Their emphasis on diversity, inclusivity and ethical company practices challenges organisations to go beyond traditional norms to meet their needs.

Gen Z is wired differently. The core values and aspirations are different, as are the expectations of how leaders should behave and communicate with them. Gen Z are the new leaders in an age of AI, of post-pandemic trauma and of dramatic climate change.

As the leaders of tomorrow, there are three core principles which these new change makers will choose to live by:

1. Commitment to positive change
2. Purpose over power
3. Courage to challenge

Arun Watkins

Arun Watkins' pace in putting big ideas into action is both brave and exceptional. In sharing his methods, I hope you are galvanised into making bigger, thinner-sliced decisions in your leadership intent.

I've known Arun since he was 11 years old, playing rugby alongside my son Tom both at their school and at Dorking Rugby Club in Surrey. Now, 14 years on, Arun is a serial entrepreneur who has completely transformed the level of participation in all forms of rugby across Britain. In many ways, he has had a better impact on the sport of rugby sevens in the past three years than the governing body, the rich and heavily-staffed Rugby Football Union, has managed in a decade.

The EggChaser brand he created has a multi-age development academy and pathway. In 2024 alone, Arun funded sports education sessions for just over 57,000 under-18-year-olds in the four countries of the United Kingdom. He has sponsored competitive teams in youth and adult rugby in tournaments in four continents, paying all flight and accommodation expenses for players and staff. This included taking 26 players to the World Youth Rugby Championship in New Zealand in December 2024 (the only British team to participate), as well as winning the international tournament at the prestigious Dubai Sevens with the senior Lionesses.

At 24 years of age, Arun is the sole owner of brands in clothing, lifestyle, sports social media and manufacturing. His portfolio includes a retail store, a production facility, a coffee brand and café, a social media company and a professional Rugby League Club (The Crusaders in North Wales). He has created a new Rugby Union Club (Horley) and two semi-professional touring sevens teams: one male and one female (Lions 7s and The Lionesses).

Arun funds his businesses by sourcing sponsors who complement the EggChaser brand and by selling modern-style sports kits he designs himself.

His vision is compelling.

> 'It's about getting kids more active. It's about increasing participation in rugby and all sport. It's about running inspiring events to promote and energise young people. We need to help schools and local communities to encourage children of all ages to be more active and less screen-led. Rugby is a good platform for us to provide events, facilities, coaches and inspiration for this ambition.'

Arun's development methods for growing participation are distinct and remarkably effective. He recruits and employs young, elite rugby players from several (mainly European and African) nations and gives them a role as the Academy's coaches. It means they have more time to practice the sport they love and, at the same time, they learn core skills faster by educating others repeatedly in those skills. These young coaches are sent to all parts of Britain to run masterclasses every week in schools and local rugby clubs.

The masterclass events are part of a pathway towards the EggChaser Academy. The training sessions are publicised on social media and through local ambassadors. The coaches have jobs in the sport they love and can train hard for competition, whilst also inspiring younger players in the sport. By using young, elite and relatable players as the coaches, participants have role models to aspire to. Through social media (26 million interactions on Instagram with the EggChaser brand over 18 months!), many more people hear about the fun masterclasses and, as a result, they attend in large numbers.

I remember one cold winter's evening arriving at Chester Rugby Club to co-ordinate the coaching team and was happily surprised to count 212 eager participants from aged seven to eighteen! In my early years as a rugby coach, I was more used to waiting for the late stragglers to make up a session of at least 10!

How Captain Arun Started

I remember watching Arun in a sprint race at his junior school and seeing a natural athlete who has what sprint coaches call a 'fast twitch' ability. Arun is naturally strong and super-fast. When he is running at full pace, he has an ability to change direction in an instant without losing momentum. This is a characteristic of only the truly elite rugby players.

As a rugby coach, I was particularly keen to observe how Arun used his natural athleticism in a contact team sport like rugby. From a young age, he brought a mental intensity to each match which indicated a stand-out combination of physical and psychological strength.

Owner Arun (far right) with the Lionesses rugby sevens team – the first women's team to win the Melrose Sevens, March 2023.

He also has an innate and distinctive propensity to focus. If the activity interests him, he brings relentless intent, energy and drive. Arun exhibits self-command, thin-slicing and positive intention in abundance.

One day in 2018, Arun invited my son Tom to form part of a team to play the small-sided form of rugby called rugby sevens, in a friendly tournament near their home club. Initially, Arun named the team the 'Lion Cubs' in homage to the British and Irish Lions team, which plays fifteen-a-side rugby on tours of the Southern hemisphere once every four years.

That first evening, reflecting on the mixed abilities of the team he had picked and played with, Arun made the decision to find a way to provide opportunities for more kids to be active in general and to play rugby in particular. He now wants to ensure that all forms of rugby develop to benefit anyone who'd like to have a go: he promotes thirteen-a-side Rugby League, fifteen- and seven-a-side Rugby Union, and has developed Kratos Rugby, a new business with aspirations to develop non-contact rugby only. Arun bought Kratos because non-contact rugby opens the sport up to many more people of all ages.

Imagine for a moment you are put in charge of a new venture which will make a positive impact on your community. What's more, there is no chance you will fail. What project would you choose? What positive impact would there be?

What are you waiting for?!

The Key Captaincy Competencies

2010 was the year I started searching for game-changing leaders in all walks of life, on my numerous travels overseas. It is why, when I post on social media, I use the hashtag *#findingleadership*. This intent was inspired by a conversation with two fellow much-travelled coaches, Kate Greaves and Philip Crocker. From our backgrounds in management and coaching, we devised a set of eight provocative, high-gain questions we would each ask of the most inspiring leaders we met.

We checked in with each other every three or four months, both to compare notes and to share the inspiring stories we were hearing and collecting from all parts of the world.

After three years, we recognised between us that there appeared to be eight consistent traits which set the really great change-makers apart from the quite good ones. We clustered these eight competencies under four sequential headings.

Visioning, Mobilising, Developing and Enabling (VMDE)

These clusters are named from the brilliant works of Ali Stewart and Derek Biddle, authors of *The Pioneer* and *Liberating Leadership*. We used the headings to frame the core behaviours required to be a game-changing Captain.

A competency is a combination of knowledge, skills and behaviour which is observable and measurable.

VISION	MOBILISE	DEVELOP	ENABLE
BRANDING	EXPLICITNESS	CONSCIOUSNESS	TRANSITIONING
Showing and growing your intrinsic self	Expressing expectations beyond doubt	Giving humble focus to self and others	Moving to a better, sustainable system
REINVENTION	TRIGGERING	TRANSFORMING	RELENTLESSNESS
Shifting paradigms which prevent growth	Initiating/driving behaviour change	Owning team capability improvement	Staying on mission until the outcome is realised

This model (using Stewart and Biddle's four phases as the base thinking) summarises neatly my leadership competency research over three decades (everything underneath the symbols). Which ones are your superpowers?

Visioning

For Missy Park, the vision behind her clothing business is wonderfully compelling: *'More active outdoorsy women, wearing clothing they love.'*

The path to most visions is often muddied, battered or even broken. The Captain needs to reinvent both themselves and their plan frequently and with ceaseless resolve; that's if they wish to see the vision come to full fruition.

Take a moment now either to check the vision you already have or set a new one. Make it easy to understand and ensure that it clearly articulates a better place than what you have now. Make sure it is easy to grasp and easy to follow. Jot some ideas down in your notebook.

One of the best examples I have seen of a vision which drives positive change in a business is the hop-on, hop-off Big Bus Tours hospitality business. Their vision is to make Big Bus Tours *'The number one thing to do in every world-famous city.'* Together with my friend and long-term colleague Amanda Downs, we sat with all the key leaders of Big Bus Tours to help facilitate the creation of this vision. When finalised, it resonated immediately with everyone because it suggests that taking the tour should be top of a tourist's to-do list, as well perhaps as the first thing they might choose to do on arrival.

It is a compelling message to all staff – drivers, tour guides and on-the-street sellers – to make sure the guest experience on their tour is amazing for all ages. It is also an easy-to-land marketing message to all tourists arriving in a major city on holiday or indeed for work... It conditions new arrivals to *'Take the Big Bus Tour as your first experience here!'*

Here's my first day in Chicago, June 2025, on the Big Bus tour with the learning champions.

Mobilising

In this phase, the competencies are explicitness and triggering.

Bringing your team, supporters and sponsors with you towards the vision is imperative. The skill of explicitness is being able to explain and sell the 'better place' that everyone should be heading towards. Explicitness is sharing, in simple words, the 'what', the 'why' and the 'so what' consequences of a message shared. Explicitness calls out the required action from the recipient(s) in no uncertain terms.

In 2010, working with my mercurial fellow coach Amanda Bennett, we took charge of an England women's rugby development squad for a week-long pre-season training camp. All the players were under the age of 25. In the first session, we covered their aspirations and our planned schedule for both the week and the competition season ahead. We then delivered an explicit, pre-prepared statement of expected behaviours and the consequences of non-compliance:

> 'With the number of high-calibre players we have here, and our bold, collective aspirations, it is essential that everyone arrives to each scheduled gathering on time and ready to practice. On time means between two and four minutes **before** the scheduled start, changed and ready to train, or ready to listen at a meeting, or just ready to eat together. If you are late for even one session without prior notice with a legitimate excuse, you will be dropped from this squad. That applies to every player and to all support staff you see in this room.'

The consequence of that explicit message was to trigger an exceptional response. Not one of the 32-strong group was late even once in the five full days together. In fact, most of the group arrived at meetings and training sessions slightly earlier than the specified time every day. Great Captains are explicit and thereby find the way to trigger positive responses to their messaging. Great Captains mobilise so that the energy is transferred from leader to the whole tribe.

Developing

This is the third phase of change-initiating leaders, involving the competencies of consciousness and transformation. These are Captains conscious of their own behaviours, ability and impact. By showing self-driven learning, they signal that evolving is an essential intention for everyone. These are the Captains who are the opposite of a *'My way or the highway'* style of authoritarian leadership.

Missy Park and the team at Title IX embody these competencies every single day. All senior team members are mentors themselves and are mentored. For some, this is 'reverse mentoring', whereby the mentor is significantly younger, bringing fresh and different perspectives.

Stop and think about that idea for a moment.

You are an advisor of those less experienced than you and at the same time receive advice from someone who is younger than you are. This reverse mentoring has high value for the mentor and mentee. I have not witnessed any examples of reverse mentoring in any traditional, hierarchical and top-down organisations.

The impact of this consciousness is to trigger capability transformation in the Captain and the team. It is the simple truth that if each individual owns their own improvement and thereby gets better at what they do, the whole atmosphere changes for the better. There's an energy you can feel when you walk into a team environment where development is a focus and an everyday occurrence.

Enabling

Enabling means setting up a new system for sustaining growth. It means the Captain is no longer needed to maintain the tribe. The two distinct competencies here are transitioning and relentlessness.

Great leaders leave a positive legacy. They enable the team to flourish in the moment and to no longer need to be led. Enabling is about creating the right environment, structure and processes to make good things repetitive and, after a while, to leave the Captain's role as more token.

Lynne Cantwell

Lynne Cantwell bringing player insights to the big strategic decisions for her sport. Photo courtesy of Lynne Cantwell.

Lynne Cantwell is a great enabler. She was a trophy-winning Captain at Richmond Rugby Club and Captain for Ireland when they won their only Six Nations Grand Slam in 2013. She remains Ireland's most capped female player and is the most recent inductee into rugby's Hall of Fame.

In 2021, Lynne took on a colossal challenge as South African rugby's first High Performance Director of women's rugby. The challenges were cultural, structural, financial and historical. Patriarchal norms often discourage women from taking up contact sports in Africa; that meant that before Lynne arrived, there was minimal media coverage, precious little funding and almost no infrastructure to help women's rugby grow.

When she left the role after four years, Lynne had created an elite coach pathway, a next-phase coach curriculum at provincial and community level, and an integration system linking girls in schools, youth academies, and the national Under-20 programme.

Please note Captains: **No system, no legacy.** When you institutionalise your programme, the Captain should be able to step away permanently with no detrimental impact on the day-to-day activities.

To an extent, Lynne is no longer needed in the South African High-Performance role because she has set up a system that is self-functioning and perpetual. She shared her reflection on the state of South African women's rugby in 2025:

> *'We've managed to empower a large cohort of women and girls who I believe will go on to be game-changers in their communities in the future.'*

During her time in South Africa, Lynne remained a board member with Sport Ireland and was chair of their Women in Sport committee. She has recently returned to Ireland to help establish similar change cohorts for her country of birth. She remains a close advisor to the South African Union to ensure that the systems she established have the right leaders in place to help them thrive.

Tracy Sweeney

Tracy Sweeney, American wine entrepreneur. Photo courtesy of Tracy herself.

The competence of transitioning is about evolving how the leader interacts with their team and how changes in the system are embedded sustainably. In Napa Valley, California, I was asked to help the hospitality team at Beringer Vineyards (part of Treasury Wine Estates) create a more welcoming atmosphere for guests who, with little wine knowledge, might feel rather intimidated by the grandeur of the property on arrival. The Beringer property is stunning visually, built in the grand Germanic style of the original brothers.

Tracy Sweeney, who was Head of the Company's Hospitality Division between 2017 and 2024, created a set of Guest Champions to own the quality of on-property customer interaction. We established a training programme for these Champions which centred on the skills of positioning, movement, rhythm and use of verbal and physical language: *'the basics, not fanciness,'* as Tracy put it. The key to sustaining this new approach was to inspire the tenured staff to become educators for all new and seasonal staff. It meant that Tracy and the leadership team could step back from the day-to-day operation and leave it to the on-site teams.

Some years after leaving the role, Tracy's legacy is that all new staff are trained on the job about guest service excellence by their colleagues from the moment they start in role. They do not have to wait for an induction programme in a classroom. An excellent guest experience is now embedded, systemised and sustained.

Paris Olympic Captains

Rugby Sevens is still a relatively new Olympic sport and yet it inspired a completely full Stade de France in Paris five days in a row, with 80,000 spectators in each of the two game sessions per day. That's approximately half a million spectators for what is still considered a minority sport. The mathematical discrepancy in this total (for all my blue energy readers) is that some people had tickets for both sessions on the same day. I was lucky to have tickets for that whole week in an iconic stadium because it showcased women's sevens just as impressively as it did for the men.

Ilona Maher

One wonderful surprise came when the US women's team won the bronze medal decider against the powerful Australian squad 14-12 with a last-minute try. In her interview after the game, Ilona Maher, a powerful 28-year-old athlete from Burlington, Vermont, spoke eloquently about how as the now most successful US rugby team in history, the women should most definitely receive parity of funding with the men. Within minutes of hearing this interview, a benefactor donated $4 million for the development of women's rugby in America.

Two trailblazers in women's rugby meet up before the 2025 World Cup.

Ilona Maher in her USA kit and Zainab Alema who famously wears a hijab head covering when she plays for Richmond Rugby Club.

Ilona has impressive physical prowess which she used effectively in a number of different competitive sports when she was young; before she took up rugby, she played softball, basketball and field hockey with standout impact. Ilona transitioned to rugby at the age of 17, inspired by her father's background in the sport. She played at college in England before transferring to Quinnipiac University, where she played a pivotal role in securing three consecutive National Collegiate Rugby Association titles (NCRA). She won the National Player of the Year deservedly.

Her call up to the national US team coincided with her introduction to TikTok as a player-reporter for all the team's exploits. She quickly found a following which grew rapidly through the pandemic and exploded after the Paris Olympics. This is tribal fire.

Today, Ilona is the most followed rugby player on Instagram and TikTok, surpassing the magnificent two-time World Cup-winning Captain from South Africa, Siya Kolisi, and the World Player of the Year and men's Olympic Gold medal winner from home-nation France, Antoine Dupont.

Ilona is a mobiliser who inspires tribal fire. She has used her athletic achievements (including finishing runner-up in the TV show *Dancing with the Stars* in 2024) to advocate for body positivity. Her social media content emphasises the importance of embracing diverse body types and promoting self-love.

When she signed for English rugby team the Bristol Bears in December 2024, the average crowd numbers on match day instantly increased from less than 2,000 to 10,000. More families attended and especially more young girls, inspired as much by her message as her sporting talent.

Ilona reflects all of the SpQ elements: thin-slicing at the post-match interview, self-command and positive intent as a player and communicator, with an impressive ability to generate tribal fire. She also personifies the eight captain competencies: the reinvention as a competitive dancer for *Dancing with the Stars*, and the explicit and relentless drive to get proper recognition and funding for women's sport.

The transformative impact of one role model like Ilona Maher, who repeatedly breaks with convention to get to a better place, is palpable.

Sam Lavelle: A True Captain Shines Brightest in Adversity

When Sam Lavelle joined Carlisle United Football Club, he was 26 and had already been a professional football player for eight years. He was signed by the then manager Paul Simpson to be the team's Captain and talisman.

We first met in pre-season training in the summer of 2023 when I spent a week with the Carlisle United players working on visioning (positive intention), self-command and tribal fire. It's great fun to facilitate goal-setting with a group of sports professionals because you see and hear all the human tendencies of hope and anxiety played out in every 40-minute team gathering.

Carlisle United had just been promoted to League 1 in England and there was trepidation in the Club's hierarchy that the squad would perhaps struggle to survive in the higher league. Many within the set-up felt that even though winning a play-off final at Wembley was a truly historic achievement, the promotion had come too soon and would put undue pressure on all aspects of the club. Sam aside, I felt that the squad lacked stand-out leaders and strength in depth.

The season started reasonably well and Sam got quickly into his stride, both as a central defender and as the new Captain. Fans in the stands could hear his voice booming encouragement to his teammates with an air of confidence and control. He was a fan favourite right from the start for his performances and his outgoing, positive energy.

From late autumn, 10 games in, the team started to falter and a poor run of results followed. With no win in 12 consecutive games, Sam's own performances started to be affected and, in tandem, his impact on his teammates reduced.

Sam texted me one Sunday morning after his mistake in the game from the previous day had gifted a decisive goal to the opponents. I had seen the reaction on social media which was pitiless in its condemnation of Sam's mistake. The majority of football fans would never openly criticise one mistake, yet the noisy and negative minority will always take to social media to berate their fallen hero. Sam was hugely self-critical in our Sunday morning discussion. He felt he was no longer worthy of a first-choice place in the team, let alone to be its Captain.

My feedback started from the premise that as an athlete, you're always as good as your best-ever game, rather than the widely-used expression that you are only as good as your last game. Sam listened and reflected. It was in that moment that he determined he would focus only on what he alone could control.

As an example, he felt he needed to be fitter and faster, so the next day he hired a personal trainer to help with what he calls *'sharpness'*. He also had separate meetings with the coaches and players to talk about team spirit and taking more personal responsibility both for fitness and performance.

Sam led Carlisle United for two seasons. The results in that period were really poor and way below expectations. Carlisle's win record was the lowest in British professional football at the time (15% over 80 matches). Despite this, Sam remained confident and positive, his voice resilient and strong with his teammates, the coaching staff and fans. Sam's reinvention and relentlessness and his mastery of self-command (SpQ) meant that despite the very real trauma all around him, Sam ended the campaign as Carlisle's and the league's highest scoring defender.

The brilliant book *The Captain Class* by US journalist Sam Walker captures Sam's leadership eloquently: *'The greatest leaders are often the ones who are overlooked – the players who grind, sacrifice and quietly lift everyone else.'*

Walker's core premise is true Captains like Lavelle are gritty, selfless and relentless. They lead through example and emotional control.

Sam reflected in a post-season debrief we had.

> 'I got more stick from fans as a player in our first season than I have seen in all my years. I guess I was taking the rap for the team's woes too. To go from there to fans' Player of the Season and "give this man a lifetime contract" in the space of six months is a good testament to my mental strength through adversity. I have just completed my counselling level 3 course because I want to be able to share my experiences for young teenagers struggling through those awkward and troubled years.'

I share Sam's story because it is not one of obvious success for the team he led. In fact, in terms of team outcomes, the opposite is true. His leadership over two years of team underperformance is a wonderful example of taking responsibility for all the things you can control; that's your self-talk, how you feel and how you role model can-do energy to teammates and management (the T.E.A.R. model in practice).

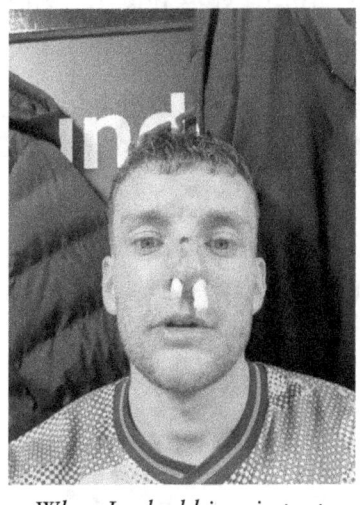

When I asked him via text 'How's your face?', he sent me this photo from the changing room. Photo courtesy of Sam Lavelle.

In one game on a blustery winter's evening, Sam broke his nose in two places in a clash with the opposition's centre forward. I know from personal experience how the body reacts to a broken nose; even trying to talk makes you wince in pain. Sam played on until the final minutes with a good result ensured.

I found being with Sam and watching him lead through adversity completely inspiring. He got stronger and Captained more maturely as the team results spiralled. He is planning to set up a business as a motivational speaker for teenagers, alongside his professional football career. I for one will be signing up for his talks.

Keep an eye on the progress of Carlisle United in the seasons to follow. It's a community club with big ambitions and role model owners, the Piatak family.

Now, take a moment to reflect on a time when the results of your hard work and effort were simply not happening, when the resistance you faced seemed insurmountable. Note down your thoughts to the following questions:

- How did you feel about continuing the endeavour?
- How motivated were you to stay positive and on task?
- How focused were you on motivating the colleagues around you to stay the course?

These are fundamental questions you need to be able to answer yourself as Sam did with *'determined, totally and very'*, as Ilona did with *'Why not?'*, and as Arun does with *'I'm just doing it!'*

The Bottom Line

Gen Z is worth listening to. They think very differently to previous generations. Are they in fact showing a smarter work/life balance?

Using Arun, Ilona and Sam's stories, and the Captain competencies they display, take time now to consider what your personal insight is from this chapter. Aim for at least one or two *Oh!* and a corresponding *And So?* for each.

OH	SO

In the next chapter, we'll cover solutions to the core question: *What's stopping you?* There is the pervading truth originally from the renowned psychologist Daniel Kahneman that nine out of ten of our thoughts and experience reflections to ourselves are negative. Is it any wonder that we tend to stay in that zone of comfort that protects us from feeling exposed or uncomfortable, and stops us from Captaining change?

Chapter 5

What's Stopping You?

Why do women suffer imposter syndrome more than men?[7]

From a young age, subtle conditioning (usually from both parents) influences girls to be humble, deferential and less assertive. It means that in adult life, the residue from that early influence can lead to a self-limiting mindset. Men are not immune, of course.

Every time I am commissioned by the United Nations to coach a Chief of Staff, I doubt my validity. I draw on my experience Captaining teams in sport where a sure voice counts, and like many of the stand-out female executives I work with, I press on, despite the negative sound of my inner voice.

---

[7] Paul C. Price, Brandi Holcomb, Makayla B. Payne, 'Gender differences in impostor phenomenon: A meta-analytic review,' *Current Research in Behavioral Sciences*, Volume 7, 2024, 100155, ISSN 2666-5182, https://doi.org/10.1016/j.crbeha.2024.100155

The Five Common Drivers

My premise is that most of what stops us happens in our own heads. In 1975, a disciple of Carl Jung called Taibi Kahler identified five common drivers that motivate (and can restrain) us (Kahler's *The Mastery of Management* is well worth a read). The drivers are born in our unconscious minds and can lead to some very positive, as well as some self-destructive, behaviour. By identifying which drivers an individual exhibits most, it becomes possible to recognise and develop the potential of these positive behaviours, and equally to respond constructively to the negative.

Below is an outline on each of these drivers:

- **Be Perfect** – doing things completely and correctly is essential.

- **Be Strong** – suck it up and don't show any weakness.

- **Hurry Up** – no dilly-dallying, always on-the-go.

- **Please Others** – never put your own interests first.

- **Try Harder** – never stop pushing for better and focus on working harder.

In reasonable quantities, these drivers are effective in creating functioning and successful individuals. But when a person is subject to too much pressure, destructive behaviours connected to the 'driver' will surface, which create stress. In Jungian terms, these are known as our 'shadow aspects'.

In his book, *Psychology and Religion: West and East*, Carl Jung wrote, 'Everyone carries a shadow and the less it is embodied in the individual's conscious life, the blacker and denser it is.'

In simple body impact terms (physiological), when we feel stress, we generate too much cortisol and our body feels the anxiousness it naturally produces.

In most people, there are two of Kahler's five drivers that are dominant in shaping behaviour. My dominant drivers couldn't have been more obvious at the start of the pandemic. Despite, or perhaps even because, we were all forced to stay at home, my 'try harder' and 'hurry up' drivers meant I was up earlier each morning, going straight online and sending email pitches to promote my remote coaching product. This was a curious approach given that most people I was trying to sell to were either off work purposefully or on government-funded furlough.

Jot down in your notebook which two of the five drivers best define what shapes your motivations. The 'be perfect' and 'try harder'' drivers, in particular, lend themselves to imposter syndrome.

2024 was a clear reinforcement for me on how the five drivers really are indicators of our entrenched habits. Within the space of six months, we moved from our 28-year family home, my first granddaughter was born, I bought a business for the first time and I had surgery to remove my cancerous prostate. Did all that slow me down like it should have done at the age of 62? Well, when there is a 'must try' harder driver, it's rather unlikely… so I started writing this book too!

I encounter far less imposter syndrome from people with a background in competitive sport, and hope that by sharing how they operate, I can show you how to be suitably fearless too. Sport teaches a core competence of style flexing – knowing when to go on attack and when to hold back and show calmness, even humility. Sport helps you learn two elements of SpQ in particular: positive intention and self-command. These are both choices rather than innate talents. You can learn them.

When Self-Command is Missing

Giannis Maniatis played 50 times for Greece including when making the last 16 of the 2014 World Cup in Brazil.

I met Giannis Maniatis in a pre-season training camp in the Greek mountains, north of Athens in August 2010. I had just been appointed mental coach for Panionios Football Club, and Giannis had, somewhat controversially, been given the Captaincy of the team.

We hit it off straight away; he was smart, passionate and suitably intense. He was also pretty angry with the management of the Greek national team, whose coach simply refused to pick 'Hothead' Maniatis. 'Manny', the nickname I have for him, was our best player by a distance so it was my job to help him channel all of his exuberant energy into purposeful play and impactful leadership. The key was to not allow his volatile emotions to detract from that mission. We worked every day on building his self-command in order to be the leader the team needed.

For the pre-season match against a team two leagues below us, I recommended that Manny sat apart from the team as we journeyed to the stadium. This was to signify that he was no longer 'one of the boys'. We sat in the front seat together and talked about how he needed to lead by his actions off the field as well as on it. He agreed this change was needed, and straight away.

When we arrived at the arena, there was a large hostile crowd which quickly surrounded our bus and started hurling verbal abuse, some bricks and what looked like chunky rocks. The angry crowd shook the bus from side to side and at one point, it felt to me like it might tip over. A police cordon created a safe corridor for us and I suggested to Manny that he should lead us off the coach with his chin up and his eyes forward.

As soon as the bus driver opened the automatic doors, Manny hurtled out and leapt over the police cordon and into the crowd, held horizontal and flailing punches wildly. Too shocked to think, I ran after him, grabbed his ankles and pulled him back into the safe passage. His eyes were bulging with anger and he said, *'They insulted my mother; it was bad!'*

When we reached the changing room, I suggested he found a quiet space to reflect and calm down. If he wanted to lead, he would need to tame his wild side deliberately and smartly.

In the game, the opposition scored first and it was Manny who equalised with a shot into the top corner of the goal from 30 yards out. He doesn't score often and as the goal was a really special piece of skill, my expectation was that he would run to the opposition fans to taunt them. Instead, he calmly jogged back towards the dugout and winked at me.

After the game, we talked about how to consistently harness his natural passion, those high emotions which by nature were always near the surface for him. We agreed that once he did, success would be inevitable for him for club and country. It was great to see him star for the Greek national team at the Brazil-hosted World Cup three years later, playing with tribal fire and mature self-command.

British Rowing Ascendency

It took an Australian coach, Paul Thompson, in the early 2000s to enable the British women's rowing eight to rise from relative obscurity to the global stage as consistent medal winners at the World Rowing Championships.

Baz Moffat was a key member of the first British women's eight to get back into the medals at the Worlds in 2007. This unleashed a decade of repeated success in the sport's blue-ribboned event for the British women's crews.

Baz Moffat.

Baz says,

> 'Competing at national level taught me that team cohesion, a smart system and personal discipline combined would pretty much guarantee positive outcomes. It most definitely gave me the bravado to co-found my business in women's health in 2021.'

Baz's business, The Well HQ, is making a profound difference in female-specific training methods across multiple sports. Baz's team of seven specialists educate athletes, coaches and sports organisations on female physiology across life stages – puberty, pregnancy and menopause.

The first three years of The Well HQ was far from smooth financially. Baz reflects:

> 'A whole bunch of goodwill about what we do, and back-slapping about my book The Female

> *Body Bible, doesn't pay the wages. At one point in 2024, we had nowhere near enough income to cover monthly staff costs. I wrote to five organisations who we dealt with and who knew us well, and spelt out we were just a few days away from closure.'*

When some great clients pre-paid for key projects, it gave Baz the breathing space to reflect on what big changes would need to be made to start to grow her business, not just survive.

> *'The best idea we had was to get a team coach at the beginning of 2025. Just like in a rowing crew, a bunch of individual stars doesn't make the boat go faster and the business coach gave us proper cohesion.'*

Baz's business model for The Well HQ is all about training managers as practitioners in schools, clubs, gyms, colleges and large sports organisations. The aim is to embed female-smart coaching routines across all athletic activity. It is exactly what has not existed in any consistent way before. This mirrors my philosophy of Champion-led change.

If Baz were back in the GB rowing team, her culture-enhancing work would see a marked shift in how female athletes would be managed; from 'push through the pain' to 'train with awareness'. It represents a mental shift required for all coaches in all sports, and it is Baz and her specialist team who lead the way.

Aisling Tuck

Aisling Tuck does not suffer from imposter syndrome, as far as I can tell. Her upbringing in Tallaght, south of Dublin, was the cornerstone for the boldness with which she approaches business. With both parents being active tennis players, Aisling inevitably took up many competitive sports, including the uniquely Irish sport of camogie – the women's counterpart to the sport of hurling, one of the world's oldest and fastest field sports. The speed and skill levels are jaw-dropping. Players use a wooden stick to strike a small ball with intensity, skill and no shortage of bravery. Make sure you find a game of camogie when you visit Ireland. It is fast, physical and all-engaging!

Camogie has empowered women in Ireland since 1904 by being integral to community life, with generations of families passionately involved every week in the same club. Despite being an amateur sport, the level of dedication feels pretty professional to me.

For Aisling, this active, outdoorsy life fostered a confidence to experiment. At 15, she turned vegetarian and at 18, fully vegan. It meant that she was cooking for herself at home and testing out a variety of plant-based recipes to satisfy her sweet tooth. Her two role models in cooking, her mum and grandmother, were mortified by how restrictive they considered veganism to be. Nevertheless, they kindly played the role of taste-testers for a multitude of what Aisling calls her 'bad' cookies. It was more than a year of experimentation before she delivered a 'brilliant' chocolate chip cookie, worthy of trying to sell.

In 2017, she founded Oh Happy Treats, offering a variety of plant-based baked goods to farmers' markets close to Dublin. At first, she cooked everything in her mum's kitchen and still has a leaning towards keeping all production in-house.

When the pandemic hit, she used the extra time it afforded to launch Naked Bakes, as well as a coffee shop in South Dublin as a showcase for her special cakes and cookies. She now has 15 staff, including a Head of Sales to expand her reach beyond Ireland.

When I asked her what her big dreams are for her business in the next five years, Aisling didn't need to think about her answer for long: *'To create a truly global brand, expanding first into the UK, then Europe and then fully global.'*

*Aisling Tuck with her rebranded Naked Bakes cookies.
Photo courtesy of Aisling Tuck.*

I asked her how she intends to make this happen. There is a sureness in her clear and confident reply:

> 'My recent rebranding and repackaging was about reflecting a brand that's growing up. From the outset, images of me on each pack was all about affirming the wholesome localness of our business. Images of me are no longer on the newest packaging. Instead, we have naked Adam and Eve images, to signify both a sense of adventure and a broader appeal.'

Take a moment to reconsider the Eight Captain competencies (page 79), both to how Aisling set up her business and how she has grown her brand and operations since. In 2025, her brand is listed by major retailers such as Lidl across Ireland, yet the product is still made at home and in a small production facility. It is also a brand that is winning countless awards for its innovation, packaging and taste. She has resisted outsourcing her production until she lands a really large customer contract to take much bigger orders in a multi-year deal.

Aisling is in the developing phase in her business, which therefore requires consciousness and transforming. She is supremely conscious of what needs to be added to her infrastructure and how her team needs to upskill for greater impact, scale and continuity. It's how the two of us first met. She signed up for a negotiation workshop through the Irish Food Board, the Dublin-based Bord Bia. I am their nominated trainer for negotiation skills alongside my brilliant Irish colleague, Malachy O'Connor.

The Bord Bia negotiation workshop is hosted by Malachy, who has a buying background, and me, representing the supplier side of the business. Aisling stated in the introduction that if she is to guarantee the future of her business as it grows, she must have the ability to hold her own when negotiating with the big retailers and wholesalers across Europe. Aisling's story is good evidence that the eight Captain competencies can be learnt, either with intentional self-command or some smart, targeted education.

Now is a good time to score yourself against these eight elements of Captain competencies (page 79). Jot down the answers to the following questions in your notebook:

- Which element is your innate strength?
- Which aspects are less strong, and yet pivotably important?
- What's stopping you putting more emphasis on what you are already good at?
- What's stopping you from making the leap in those development areas?
- Do you need a mentor to help with that self-reflection?

Aisling had two key mentors during the formative years of her business: her mother and her grandmother. Seeking a mentor to share perspective, experience and supportiveness is a smart way to grow Captain competency, especially when your thoughts are self-limiting or imposter syndrome debilitates you. Ask yourself:

'Who is, or could be, my best mentor now?'

Chin-Ning Chu

I had the great good fortune of being sought out by a mentor soon after I had started my consultancy business in 2002. Whilst I was supposedly in charge of all the speakers at a leadership conference in Sardinia that summer, I soon recognised that the headline speaker, Chin-Ning Chu (all 4 foot 11 inches of her), would be calling all the shots.

In my conference compère duties, as Chin-Ning Chu was the keynote speaker, I rang her as my first task a good fortnight before the event. We shared the agenda and conference theme, and I was surprised that she seemed fully prepared already. She walked me through both her intended opening speech and her closing keynote too. I congratulated her on her readiness and suggested that given an afternoon start for the first day, perhaps we could meet on the morning of the conference for breakfast and a rehearsal. Chin-Ning retorted instantly:

> 'You need to arrive on the afternoon before that as I will be taking you out to dinner to get to know you properly. No need to bring your wallet; I shall be covering all costs at a special restaurant I have visited before on the island. It's my treat!'

I was blown away by this bold signal that relationship matters more than the task (it wasn't my natural way of working at the time!).

Chin-Ning Chu was born in China in 1947, and within six years had moved to Taiwan with her family as refugees. It was perhaps this turmoil which inspired her father to choose *The Art of War* by Sun Tzu as regular bedtime reading for his only child. I asked Chin-Ning how old she was when he first read it to her. She replied with a wry smile, *'I think I was four!'*

At our first face-to-face meeting, Chin-Ning said she applied the main principles of *The Art of War* to every part of her life. As an example, she was the best table tennis player in her school because, unlike the other pupils, she had a pre-planned strategy and played only to her strengths and to the observed weaknesses in her opponents. She said she enjoyed beating the boys especially because their arrogance always got in the way of their shot choice and execution. *'Play with their heads and they crumble,'* she reflected gleefully.

Chin-Ning then turned her attention to me and shared some extraordinary observational feedback.

> *'You walk fast and breathe shallow. It shows you have a high "can-do" energy, and yet your brain will crave more oxygen to match the physical exertion that you are giving it. In the conference this week, please focus your preparation on repeated deep breathing. This will calm and clear your mind when you speak; your natural energy will still shine through, and your voice will have a deeper resonance.'*

I followed Chin-Ning's guidance deliberately that week and I felt the audience were more captivated than in all my previous experiences as an on-stage speaker. I was calmer and bolder after those pre-speaking deep breathing exercises. With an audience of 250, I finished the final plenary session by wishing everyone *'safe travel*

*Chin-Ning Chu – author, speaker and amazing mentor.
Photo courtesy of JT International.*

home' and then asking them to stand up and sing the first two lines of Queen's anthem *Fat Bottomed Girls* together:

*Are you gonna take me home tonight?
Oh, down beside that red firelight*

All that extra oxygen had clearly emboldened me.

Chin-Ning was laughing so much in the front row that she couldn't sing.

On reflection, walking fast and breathing shallow are innate behavioural traits in me which are clear signs that I have a 'hurry up' driver. No time to think or plan – just 'let's go!' Her feedback helped me improve my self-command, both at work and in my sport, where I was Captain at CERN St Genis Rugby Club into my early forties.

I still use Chin-Ning's advice, especially when my heart rate increases just before I start speaking to a large audience, or if I feel a little bit anxious with the volume and urgency of my to-do list.

My favourite of Chin-Ning's books is *Thick Face, Black Heart*. 'Thick face' is about emotional resilience; cultivating the ability to endure criticism, rejection and failure without letting those imposters impact your self-worth or determination to proceed. 'Black heart' is about mastering the balance between compassion and toughness; it's about making the tough, unpopular decisions with courage and resolution. It is important to stay true to your values and to the belief that the decisions made are for the good of all.

> *'How much do I need to challenge?*
> *How much support do I need to give and get?'*

These are great introspective questions for you as you seek to lead. For me, I needed an external agent to help me find those answers – Chin-Ning would love me describing her as an external agent, as she always said she wanted one day to appear in a James Bond film.

Take a moment to reflect who should be, and can be, a mentor on your journey. Jot your ideas down in your notebook. Try and think of three credible options.

If you are aged 40 or over, consider taking on a reverse mentor, someone like Arun Watkins or Aisling Tuck. Someone from a much younger generation than you will inevitably have a wholly different perspective on the world. They would most definitely bring a fearlessness that may help you be more courageous in your decision-making. I am already taking my lead from my granddaughter Lavinia Jay – mainly mirroring her exploratory and fearless body language.

Although I never met Chin-Ning in person again after our Sardinian adventure, every Chinese New Year she would send me an inspirational card in the post, inviting me, amongst other things, to be bolder, to take calculated risks and to inspire others to show leadership in areas they could and should influence. When we moved countries, I sent her my change of address and she carried on the New Year tradition until the year she died in 2009. Every Chinese New Year, I take a moment to consider what she would have written to me. It's never the same and it remains a super legacy from a true Captain; she was a special author, business strategist and motivational speaker. Above all else, she was a kind and characterful mentor for me.

Julia Conway

Julia Conway was born into the bus and tourism business on the east coast of America. The Conways are synonymous with bus travel and her dad was her first key mentor, instilling in the whole family a work ethic which still drives Julia today. From her early teenage years, she was introduced to all aspects of the business: mechanic, driver, tour guide, seller and financial cash manager.

This was to serve her well when personality clashes within the family inspired her to set up her own tour business, in competition with her father and brothers, of course! It meant Julia transitioned rapidly into a leadership position which has, by my observation, challenged her imposter syndrome tendencies ever since. For me and her eager followers, the self-deprecation and humility just adds to her radiant charm.

Julia is commercially savvy and business-focused in a people-centric way. She leads in a spontaneous, energetic, authentic and fun-loving style. Julia is easy to follow.

When she was asked to set up Big Bus in New York in 2013 by Pat Waterman, the brilliant Group CEO based in the London head office, Julia considered it as *'One last challenge before I retire to my dream home in Miami.'* More than a decade later, she is the Group COO, leading a $300 million business and Big Bus tours in 32 of the world's most famous cities.

Julia (middle) presenting certificates to Champions: Pania (from Sydney Big Bus) and Claudia (Madrid team).

When Julia sits in her office on the fifth floor of the building, opposite the M&M store on New York's 7th Avenue, she gets a bird's eye view of Bus Stop 1 for her fleet.

There are times when the queue to board the next bus snakes around the corner. That's when Julia sense-checks how her on-the-street team leader is engaging and reassuring the guests. Blink and you'd miss her bounding across the street to pronounce, *'Hi folks, I'm Julia. I have checked that the next bus is just three minutes away and as I am a driver, you can choose which one of us you'd prefer to see in the driver's seat!'*

You can take operations out of the Captain but you can never take a true thin-slicing Captain completely out of being operational when the situation demands!

You'll have recognised a number of key characteristics in all of these Captain stories. To be a significant change instigator is obsessive hard work. If that simply isn't in your DNA, you might as well stop reading this as a self-improvement book. However, please continue to enjoy the stories and share them with at least one friend who has relentlessness in their locker.

The Bottom Line

1. Know what your main drivers are and how they can motivate or restrict you.

2. Choose a mentor who can help trigger new actions (can be a younger, reverse mentor).

3. Be conscious of the change sequence, VMDE – which stage are you at?

Reflect on what's stopping you doing what you want. Is it your inner critic? Is it outside voices? Is it imposter syndrome? What's your biggest *Oh!* and crucially, what's the *And So?*

OH	SO

In the next chapter, we will provoke you to 'Get visible!' so there'll be no imposter syndrome when we ignite your social media presence. It highlights all the key aspects to formulate your message and how best to communicate it for impact and adoption.

Chapter 6

Get Visible (Share the Good Stuff!)

Approximately 50 British women have reached the summit of Mount Everest. In 2025, 20 of them gathered for a reunion to mark 50 years since the diminutive Japanese climber Junko Tabei paved the way for others. Junko was the first woman to reach the summit of the world's tallest mountain.

Bonita Norris

In 2012, 22-year-old Bonita Norris became the youngest British female to climb the world's tallest mountain. In the following year, she became the youngest person ever to reach both the North Pole and the summit of Everest. At the time of writing, this record still stands.

The red thread in this chapter is Bonita's philosophy when she is climbing precarious heights: *'Find the good stuff'* and share it with others.

The Captaincy

When Bonita Norris climbs, she sees the world very differently than most people get to experience, August 2025. Photo courtesy of Bonita Norris.

Bonita explains this mindset in her motivational speeches. She talks of the slog, hard work, exhaustion, boredom and challenge in mountaineering. That makes it vital for self-preservation that you stay alert to and for the 'really good stuff' moments: those moments which may not be noticed if you are merely grinding on, slogging your heart out, with your head firmly down.

On the gruelling final assault on the Everest summit in the death zone, one of Bonita's fellow climbers simply said to her, *'Look up!'* The stars, in a suddenly cloudless sky, were engulfing the climbers' position, as if they were in the middle of the panoply rather than below it as all non-climbers usually experience. That's the epitome of sharing the good stuff!

When Bonita was 21, she heard Kenton Cool speak at the Royal Geographical Society. It was at that moment she decided to have a go at Everest herself, despite having absolutely no climbing experience or any independent funds to invest in the project. You need at least £50,000 to cover all the costs of climbing the world's tallest mountain, and Bonita tried for a full, exhausting year to find sponsors for her attempt. It was *'No'* at every turn. Just when she was about to give up, she tried one last call, this time to a radio station, and managed to get live on air. By chance, it triggered a corporate sponsor to fund her whole Everest expedition.

I first met Bonita when she was presenting her remarkable Everest story at the 2023 Majestic Wine Annual Leaders' Conference at Epsom Racecourse in Surrey. I was impressed by her style of communication as well as the spellbinding stories she told. I waited for her to leave the stage to take a tea break so that I could introduce myself and offer some feedback on how well she had presented and a couple of tips to be even better.

In our discussion, she shared that being a motivational speaker was still really new for her and she had only started it because she wanted something active to keep her occupied while she took a break from climbing; it would keep her busy while she stayed at home with her young kids *'for at least a few weeks.'*

I invited Bonita to speak at a business leaders' conference which is hosted twice a year by my company, Uspire. I encourage you to follow Bonita on LinkedIn; she posts twice a week, sharing her insights on the speakers' circuit as the Storyteller of the Year 2025.

Bonita Norris smiling at the summit of the treacherous Matterhorn, August 2025 (4,478 metres) in under four hours – a sprint compared to Everest (twice the height). Photo courtesy of Bonita Norris.

Bonita has five top tips for Champions to be successful in life:

1. Start – whatever it is you want to achieve, stop procrastinating and begin.
2. Visualise – see yourself successful.
3. Get into nature – to clarify your thoughts.
4. Clear your ego out of the decision-making – be honest and vulnerable.
5. Trust – in *something*, or just in yourself.

Smart Social Media

When you consider your messaging on social media, think first about who your target audience is. It's just lazy to think it's anyone who might be interested. Be specific about who and why you want them to be your audience. Then, when deciding what to share with them, use Bonita's mantra: *'Find the good stuff'*. It should be about how what you do is relevant, interesting and valuable to your target audience.

I vlog (visual blog) twice a week passionately about wine, sport and/or leadership. To find valuable content worth sharing online, I aim to seek out the winemaker in each vineyard wherever I am, and find something different and unusual to mention in a short iPhone-generated video.

As a result of these social media messages, more than 30% of my new clients over the last 18 months have been in the wine industry. My target audience on LinkedIn is clearly watching my posts and interested. They tell their friends and my followship grows. I try to be spontaneous too and when the mood grabs me, I turn the iPhone on myself and start speaking as if chatting to a friend. Smile, turn the video on and project!

As *The New Fire* by Nick Francis suggests:

> 'When it's done right, video can move people emotionally and make them act. That's power – and that's why we call it "the new fire".'

Getting visible is a vital enabler for Captains who want to impact a wider audience.

Nicki Drinkwater

*Nicki Drinkwater.
Photo courtesy of Nicki.*

Nicki Drinkwater (née Jupp) was a trophy-winning Captain for Richmond Rugby Club in 2005–2006 and an England international from 2000–2004. When she emigrated to Australia in 2010, she retained her competitive interests both in team and individual events. She took the leadership and communication qualities learnt on the sports field into sports management and then drinks manufacturing, before a defining move into a high-stakes public sector role for the national broadband network (nbn) in Australia.

Nicki was nbn's General Manager, Media and External Communications, during Covid – just when the rapid expansion of online meetings for nearly all white-collar jobs became a global imperative, and when fast, reliable digital connectivity became an essential service, supporting remote working, telehealth and online education.

The key elements of her highly-regarded strategy are worth noting and embracing:

- Have a clear narrative – understand your story. What is it that makes you uniquely you, that sets you apart from others? What will you be known for?

- Listen to your audience – understand them. What are their needs and wants? What do they expect of you?

- Identify your strategic messaging pillars – and use this to create a master messaging framework. Be specific – for each of the core pillars of your narrative, what are the explicit benefits for your audience? Remember, *'People don't care what you do, they care why you do it'* (Simon Sinek).

- Engage with authenticity and purpose – every engagement with others, every communication, is a chance to tell your story. Be purposeful in your messaging, and authentic in your storytelling. Stay true to yourself.

I reckon this is a decent ambition list for anyone wishing to master their own messaging.

Kelly Fidler

Kelly Fidler. Photo courtesy of Kelly.

Canadian Kelly Fidler began her career inside the four walls of a hospital as a medical technologist.

She quickly realised that her passion lay in connecting people to purpose, not just products. With a career spanning diagnostics, medical devices and pharma, she built a dynamic track record in sales, marketing and executive leadership across start-ups, mid-size, and Fortune 100 companies. We know each other from working in Toronto together when she was Head of Sales for Edwards Canada, where I witnessed her bold human-first leadership style.

I knew Kelly would have great insight about getting visible as a woman in the corporate world and these are some fascinating reflections:

> 'I thought at first if I just did the work, someone would notice. For years, I believed:
>
> *talent + hard work = recognition*
>
> *Simple, right?*
>
> *But somewhere along the way, I realised visibility is part of the job. Not in a shout-it-from-the-rooftops kind of way (ugh), but in a strategic, intentional own-your-impact kind of way.*

> *Turns out the people who get ahead aren't always the best – they're often just the best at making sure their work is seen, heard and felt by the right people. I still cringe at shameless self-promotion, but I am warming up to the idea of sharing value, not just creating it.'*

This advice from Kelly really resonates with me in terms of how I use LinkedIn as a value-sharing platform. I post about subjects I know a decent amount about: sport, wine and leadership. Consequently, at least once in each working day, someone will thank me for the insight I share about the wines I encounter on my travels. It means my LinkedIn communication is sharing stories and insights which resonate with a like-minded business audience.

For my business, it has established a degree of credibility in that space. I train in the wine sector, and extensively in multiple industries. I specialise in sales and presentation skills, team management and leadership.

If you were to take a moment now to dial my mobile, you'll likely get my answerphone message. It's always upbeat, enthusiastic and will have a sign-off which implores you to:

> 'Leave a message and in the meantime, have a FAN-TAS-TIC day!'

Notice that it is directly reflective of the core details in my brand key: *'Infectious enthusiasm and positive impact'*. It means that some of my contacts say to me that when they are feeling down, they call my mobile and hope I don't reply so they can get a boost from listening to my ceaselessly positive message!

Kelly Fidler's top tips on getting visible are worth documenting and following:

1. **Master the invisible curriculum.** Every workplace has two rulebooks: the official one, and the one people don't talk about. Learn how things really get done. See who gets heard and learn why. That's not selling out; it's smart navigation. (See how Charlie Bronks navigates smartly in the banking world in Chapter 7.)

2. **Relationships move decisions.** Build trust before you need it. Advocate for others so that they learn to advocate for you. It's not networking; it's strategic generosity.

3. **You need sponsors, not just mentors.** Mentors give advice. Sponsors put their name on the line for you. One conversation can change your year. One sponsor can change your life.

4. **Start documenting your impact relentlessly.** Don't wait for a performance review to prove your value. Build your evidence file. Track results. Capture praise. Advocate with facts, not feelings.

5. **If the room doesn't see your worth, ask yourself if it was built to.** You may not be the problem. But you are responsible for protecting your potential. Sometimes, the boldest move is to walk away from systems which feed on silence.

When Covid hit in 2020, my consultancy business was left without a foreseeable revenue source. We chose to get busy ('try harder' driver) by hosting a podcast to raise money for the NHS. We decided to call the programme 'Boostcast' with £1 donated for every listener who clicked in to join the 'boost'. In the 29 shows, we attracted just over 31,000 views and the corresponding funds meant we generated enough money to donate to three separate NHS staff support projects in London and the Midlands.

Presenting the cheque from the Boostcasts to Jennie Pearce from Barts Hospital Charity. Photo courtesy of the Uspire Partnership.

Riffi Khan

One of our Boostcast guests had been reluctant at first to be interviewed on the programme. Successful TV producer Riffi Khan has been creating some of the most popular TV shows on English television from behind the camera for the last 20 years. Shows like *I'm a Celebrity Get Me Out of Here*, *Come Dine With Me* and *Hell's Kitchen* have been award-winning, multi-year successes. Nevertheless, being the centre of attention in front of the camera was never on Riffi's agenda. She shared her thoughts on this on Boostcast:

> *'Being in front of the camera and getting my own voice out there has never been an intention of mine. In fact, I had refused to even consider it an option until I was asked to speak at a conference called Rise, to help women who struggled with imposter syndrome to break out from that self-limitation. As that self-imposed reticence sounded like me, I just thought, why not just go for it?'*

Here's Riffi as an interviewee for a BBC documentary. Photo courtesy of Riffi Media Ltd.

Riffi continued:

> *'For me, there's a constant battle with the ego internally; am I so special that I should turn up, speak up and share what I have learnt in my life – just to stroke my ego – or should I use introversion as an excuse to avoid showing up at all, making myself the focus by hiding? I have learned to balance that with, "OK, I*

have had a life and maybe there is something in what I have to say that might be of value to those listening" – *it's not for me to judge or limit myself. The audience get to decide; all I have to do is show up and be fully myself. This is how I managed the move from interviewing others strictly behind the camera, to being in front of the camera when opportunities came. I love interviewing and it's a privilege holding a space for others whilst they relay their story.*

Everybody has a unique story. One that is interesting and worth hearing and will resonate with someone, even if it's for one person – the domino effect is powerful. Having the courage to speak your truth can be offloading and cathartic for you and others. It's always a symbiotic energy exchange. Start by sharing your story a few times with a variety of friends who respect you and will listen (not the naysayers in your social group). This will build your confidence and then, step-by-step, you are ready to become a true change-maker by sharing your voice beyond your friend group and create impact. I believe in "What you are seeking is seeking you".

The second bit is being smart with time and energy. Ensure you are using your voice on the right platforms. Do you feel a calling as a female change-maker? Do you want to make the world a better place? Are there things you see in the world that are unacceptable to you and that cross your boundaries? Then step up and do something about it, but on the highest level possible. Make yourself seen and heard where it counts. Show up, at that highest level – it takes the same time and energy as showing up small. By the highest level, I mean speak at government select committees, the national press and the courts. You have nothing to lose going for the seats at tables that carry weight, change policy and have impact. In the era of noise and influence, being your authentic self will always cut through.

When you need to step up to a new or bigger out-of-comfort audience, imagine you are talking to yourself in the most beautifully kind and free way – no self-edits. I find if I prepare in this way, the right words flow and the message shared is both easy to listen to and entirely authentic.'

Riffi also shared her advice about how to become a storyteller to a wider community:

'Words are the most powerful tool in the world so the words we choose are simply vital; a few words can destroy someone, and a few choice words can build someone up.

1. *Once you have a story you are passionate about, share it with someone you trust to sense check it with, before you take it to a wider audience.*

2. *Be ready to be uncomfortable – it's normal and means you're growing.*

3. *Show up – it's safe to be visible.*

4. *Follow your light – it's bursting inside you.'*

Brand You

I hope Riffi's words have triggered you to consider you as a brand. In my LinkedIn profile, the first description you'll see and read is that I am a 'Dolphin trainer'. This is both a core philosophy and a deliberately unusual expression of my profession. Unsurprisingly, it generates a lot of interest and questions, including *'Are you really a dolphin trainer?'* I usually reply, *'Well, yes, in a way, I am!'* and then I tell the following story.

My Why Story

The Miami heat was stifling. I was waiting at the side exit of the performance arena at Sea World for what seemed like a lifetime. When the dolphin trainer appeared, I just blurted out the question without so much as a *'Hello'*:

'How did you make her do that last trick? It was amazing!'

'Oh, don't worry, she does what she wants to do: it hasn't got much to do with me!'

I still needed to know more and asked, *'Does she do it for the fish you give her after each trick?'*

'Nope, those are thank-yous, not rewards: dolphins just like to make their friends happy!'

It has taken me a few decades to finally understand how profound those words were, freely given to the eight-year-old me. If there's no trust, there are no tricks. If there is no trust, no magic happens.

In my first corporate role assignment straight out of university, I was made an Assistant Brand Manager for a beer called Boddingtons of Manchester. This was a pretty cool first project in my early twenties, because we were given the task of helping make a regional brand from North West England the nation's favourite traditional beer.

We knew that one of the unique selling points (USP) was the size and creaminess of the white froth on top of the liquid. As a result, in early 1991, Barrie Boyle from our advertising agency crowned the phrase the 'Cream of Manchester' for an advertising campaign which is still remembered in Britain today. We made the USP 'creaminess' the visual representation of our message and it catapulted our sales exponentially.

I won't go into more marketing speak now, other than to suggest that if your message matters, it needs to be heard. If it needs to be heard, then you need to be clear and explicit about who you are and what value you have to share. For that, I recommend first that you create your own 'brand key'. This is to help you emphasise the good stuff and to refine your Captain's message.

Right in the centre of my brand key are the words, *'Infectiously enthusiastic and positive impact'*. If you see my LinkedIn posts, you'll see and feel that energy. I know the brand I wish to be and to portray, which also means I don't post negative thoughts about anybody. It would be incongruent with my brand essence.

Your brand key is the framework for consistent messaging and visual identity across all touchpoints, from the spoken work and digital communication to your social media presence. The idea of a brand key comes original from Robert Passikoff (1984) and then adapted for each of its consumer brands by the Unilever corporation. I have adapted the idea for personal branding. Here's the version I use as a coaching tool, ideal for you to complete.

Grab your notebook and draw the image below. You can start right in the middle circle or at the bottom of the key and work up. This may be slow going at first – deep thinking required, but stick at it!

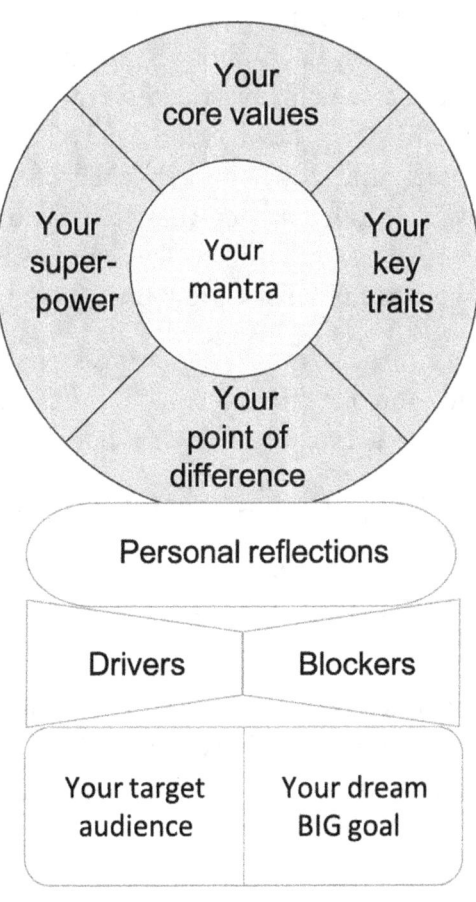

Now you have clarity about you as a brand, take a pause for a moment and embrace an idea I stumbled on in Paso Robles, Central Coast, California in the summer of 2024.

The scrumptious coffee emporium called Spearhead – incidentally using a coffee-roasting machine made in 1947! – adorned its walls with photographs of entrepreneurial women from the local area.

The series of images are called '40 over 40' by Californian photographer Allyson Magda Rivera. Her work focuses on capturing the essence of individuals in moments of time. Each photo has a short biography under the frame which investigates how the subject's values have shifted as they have journeyed through life, how they mark milestones and checked off bucket list items. They also offer advice that they would give to their 20-year-old self. Four coffees in, I was reading each bio twice as fast! They are truly inspiring.

Now it's your turn. Why not get a professionally-created portrait and attach a short, inspiring biography? It is a different way to get visible. Here's what you do:

1. Hire a photographer to take a top-class photo of you.

2. Frame it with a short story of why what you do is special.

3. Take it to the best coffee shop in your town and persuade them to showcase it! (If just one photo seems weird, entice them to start a competition using your example!)

The Bottom Line

The chapter started at the top of Everest asking its hardy climbers *'Where's the really good stuff in this venture?'* With examples from Bonita, Nicki, Kelly and Riffi, make a start on getting your brand out there with a purpose.

Grab your notebook and answer three key questions:

- Who is my target audience for my big dream/product/service offering?

- What is the value I provide, both factually and emotionally?

- What is the core message I would like to deliver?

Make a note of your learnings from this chapter in the *OH* below and your goals in the *SO*.

OH	SO

In the next chapter, I'll share how to create a following of like-minded, passionate people who will assist you in landing your vision.

Chapter 7

Gather Your Tribe

Anthony Willoughby is an eccentric British adventurer who has spent the past 50 years navigating some of the world's most remote and rugged landscapes – both geographic and human – in a quest to discover what makes leadership authentic and meaningful.

His life's work began at 22 with a one-way ticket on the Trans-Siberian Railway, followed by a boat trip to Yokohama, Japan. Since then, Anthony has wandered across the Taklamakan Desert in China, climbed the 7,546m Muztagh Ata in Western China solo, without oxygen, AND recently joined nomadic herders on camels during their annual migration through the -30°C wilderness of Western Mongolia.

These wild adventures led to something deeper.

Over decades of conversations with indigenous leaders and nomadic communities, Anthony began to notice something profoundly simple and universal. People who knew their *territory* and what they were *hunting*, *protecting* and *growing* had a stronger sense of direction, confidence and contribution. They didn't chase trinkets. They didn't waste time complaining. They lived with clarity and relevance. Each member of the tribe mattered and felt their worth with the collective.

Drawing from these insights, Anthony developed Territory Mapping (territorymapping.pro) – a visual tool and methodology that helps people reconnect with their inner compass. Mapping has been embraced by leaders and corporations all over the world, including Ferrari, Virgin and Dyson. Even the Bill & Melinda Gates Foundation uses mapping to drive their philanthropic causes.

I work with Anthony and his Japanese-based team to provide my clients with a truly different leadership experience, helping them to access the caveman and woman behind the computer.

In recent weeks, Anthony has developed AI Territory Mapping so you can use smart software to help broaden and sharpen your strategic thinking. It's certainly helping the leaders I work with to find more options to navigate increasingly crowded, complex and confused territories.

Emmanuel Mankura

It was through Anthony that I met Emmanuel, a tribal elder and cultural ambassador for the Maasai people. This was a special privilege for me as my dissertation at university was on the Maasai tribes' responses to European colonisation.

I asked Emmanuel, *'What are the key components of a sustainable tribe?'*

His thoughtful and impactful response was:

Cultural Ambassador Emmanuel Mankura. Photo courtesy of Nomadic Wisdom Ltd.

> *'Can you be trusted? Can you imagine a life whereby nobody trusts you? Do you deserve to be trusted? We have a Maasai proverb that says "If I cannot trust you with a small thing, then actually how can I trust you with a big thing?" I believe that trust is in the middle; it is in the centre. It is in the centre of life in our community, so without trust, we stop living. We start to die.'*

Anthony Willoughby builds on these thoughts insightfully:

> *'Many people have gone through their lives thinking that they are self-actualising because they have "Director" in their title and a BMW in the garage. They have built their lives on structure, status and stability in the belief that is the key. That type of stability simply doesn't exist. It is a pure figment of people's imagination. In the Maasai, whether you are a man, a woman, a girl or a boy, your responsibilities have to keep pace with your level of contribution. And the concept is that every single person in the community is a leader. The smallest child, looking after goats, is leading. That is the core*

concept of leadership. You have to realise that leadership is the ability to contribute.'

When Covid gripped the world, my training business, which was reliant on face-to-face education, was instantly paralysed. As a small team, we used Anthony's Territory Mapping concept to first and foremost keep our tribe alive and then to reframe our whole proposition. Here is the territory map drawn by Jonathan Brough, who is my stepbrother and mercurial business partner. It gives you a great sense of the challenges and aspirations of our business in the early months of Covid.

Image courtesy of Jonathan M. Brough.

Establishing, leading and inspiring followers is what great Captains do.

I love watching how communities assemble, co-habit and grow together, enabled by a shared experience and ideally a leader with vision. This chapter highlights the crucial role the Captain plays in the *forming*, *storming*, *norming* and *performing* phases of a tribe. The Captain is both the initiator of tribal fervour and, in the early days, a needed bonding agent.

In my experience, the richest communities are tangibly diverse, and they welcome multifarious talents, attitudes and personalities. When diversity is observed, respected and embraced, magic happens both within the tribe and because of it.

A Tribal Story

Back in the spring of 2018, my friend and neighbour Seb Watts (whom I also knew through our sons' local school in Surrey where Seb was Deputy Head) asked me if I would join him at a local complaint-handling section of a council meeting.

We needed to protest against the lack of action to repair a badly potholed road near where we lived. The key issue was that the road led to Woodlands School, a school for children with special educational needs; a seriously rough and bumpy road meant an unacceptably unpleasant ride twice a day for the children, many with significant frailties.

At the council meeting, we were told that the road was 'unadopted' and therefore not the council's responsibility. They echoed that whilst they had great sympathy for our cause, their own long-established legislation forbade them to take any action.

I was surprised and incensed by this abdication of responsibility, so I interrupted the summation by the council leader to appeal directly to the 80-strong group in the public gallery: *'Don't you all think we need to run a campaign to get this nonsense sorted fast?'*

Stephen Dyke, the Head of Mencap in Mid-Surrey, replied, *'Yes! It needs a leader to organise us and to get people to be vocal enough to be disruptive. I would recommend you, Mark, to lead it.'*

Seb, my beacon here, smiled knowingly as several voices coerced an *'OK then'* response from the neatly railroaded me! A beacon is more than a light in the distance; it's a promise, unwavering in its purpose. A beacon doesn't chase the darkness away, but shines in spite of it. A beacon enables positive change. Seb was my beacon.

The tribe for our campaign grew fast. Within a week, we had 1,500 protester signatures requesting an emergency meeting of the full council. We formed an eight-strong action committee, which invited all forms of media to hear our voice.

With national television coverage for our cause imminent, the council surprisingly and rapidly changed their minds! They funded a complete and fast repair of the road, which they formally 'adopted' as well (this means repairs and upkeep will be their responsibility in perpetuity).

This new, bonded and recently victorious tribe vowed to be available whenever a significant local issue surfaced again. We determined that any issue which we felt would require a coordinated response would trigger the need to reassemble the tribe. We reunited during the early months of the pandemic to assist making home deliveries for those in our community with underlying health issues and most at risk from the virus.

When I am the Captain, my prime focus is to create a community with shared aspirations. When I run pre-season training for professional football teams, I use every fun, taxing and illuminating team-building exercise I can remember. None have much, if anything, directly to do with football, except blindfold penalties, which are hilarious. We make the team-building exercises competitive, of course. I also share the colour energy personality profiles of everyone in the squad and management team. We discuss, we laugh and we determine how we want to behave with each other. These purposeful exercises bond disparate people. They enlighten. They set the tone.

Take a moment to reflect on which communities you're a member of and jot them all down. Now decide what their stated or implicit purpose is. Consider what your role is within each one. Are you an inactive passenger, such as not participating in your Neighbourhood Watch scheme? Are you a Captain now in any tribes? Consider which tribes you could be the Captain for.

I have two insightful stories of great tribal Captains whom I know now as friends: Charlie Bronks, a leader and influencer in the banking sector, and Aduke Onafowokan, founder of The Sister Sister Global Network (now known as the Horizon Collective). I have had the privilege of coaching them both and watching them soar. They exhibit a higher purpose in their intention, focus and daily behaviours.

The descriptor of 'role model' is often applied to Charlie and Aduke. I prefer to see them as 'beacons' – the unwavering purpose and inner strength that Charlie and Aduke's investors, stakeholders and followers cherish most.

In a world often shrouded in uncertainty, become a beacon who enables positive change. Establishing, leading and inspiring followers is what great Captains do, even if, initially, they are completely alone.

Charlie Bronks

It was a real treat catching up with Charlie to talk about her success in the ESG side of the banking world (environmental, social and governance). We know each other because I coached her first in her teenage years at Richmond Rugby Club in the early 1990s, right through her performances for the world-conquering England women's rugby team. Charlie was a member of the first England team to win the Women's Rugby World Cup in Edinburgh in 1994.

In our discussion, she recounted that her sporting career has been a great foundation for success in the corporate world.

This is Charlie Bronks on one of her many stage appearances.

'I knew I wasn't the best player in my chosen position so I needed to make myself a more versatile player, to at least make sure I was in the wider squad based on breadth of ability, not just one position specialism. I play in the front row and had expertise as a hooker and a tight head prop. If I could learn to play at loose head prop too, I would bring a relatively rare set of competencies to the England set-up. I approached Jason Leonard who was, at the time, the best player in my position in the world (and a world cup winner himself with England in 2003).

Jason made me more technically smart in the dark arts of playing as a front rower; he showed me little tricks and tips to put my opponent in an awkward, more vulnerable position. Shortly after his help, I was picked to play for the Nomads team against England in a warm-up game ahead of the 1994 World Cup. This was just before the selection for England's tournament squad. I was able to switch my position to demonstrate to the selectors I had strengths in more than one role. I was able to apply what I'd learned because I was genuinely enjoying that challenge. I received the letter as a selected player straight after the match, with the World Cup in Scotland just around the corner.

Next, I made sure I turned up to any trial or England training session with the best, most open and positive attitude. It was more than simple eagerness; it was a purposeful mindset, adaptable and helpful.'

Charlie always exudes an overtly positive energy and intention, which is a central aspect of SpQ and her brand essence.

So much of what sport teaches is transferable into a business setting. How to be resilient; how to cope under duress; how to be a teammate or a team motivator. In sport, Charlie smartly found partners in her quest for international recognition. She was forthright in asking for advice and help. She was also a great person to have in a squad of players because she was always smiling, encouraging and driven.

She is now a prominent figure in finance, serving as the group head of sustainability at Crown Agents Bank. It's a role she created herself when she saw that the business needed a clearer approach to the non-financial aspects of its existence (otherwise known as a balanced scorecard). She sold the concept of creating both an internal and external communication strategy to her board. Her pitch highlighted to the executive team that being seen as a leader in sustainability and corporate responsibility would be both a commercially sound decision and a means to enhance the bank's reputation and talent attractiveness, based on demonstrable integrity.

For the first two years, Charlie worked on the ESG project for her bank as a sole contributor driving this profound culture change. Her Captaincy was clearly a beacon driving change.

Charlie's tribe is growing both internally and well beyond her professional endeavours. She is an active member of the United Nations Global Compact Network (UNGC), serves on the advisory board for ESGmark®, and is co-chair of the Payments Association. She is also a regular podium speaker on sustainability and ESG topics.

So, how does a woman lead in a male-dominated environment?

> '*Step one: I talk "male,"*' Charlie answers my question with a smile.
>
> '*Not unlike how you talked "woman" to the players when you coached us at Richmond. You were in every sense one of us, with no sense of detachment, superiority or sexual innuendo. We had a shared goal to be the very best, and we achieved it consistently (European Champions four years in a row!) and 60 women and you and Simon breathed, worked and triumphed as one.*
>
> *I find switching into talking "male" easy. I have three brothers and a rather traditional dad. Add*

that to my passion for sport, and there's the foundation which usually disarms any initial conversational tension with blokes. Thereafter it's about really knowing and adapting my style and tone to my audience, irrespective of their background, mindset or sexual orientation. I translate my solution idea into what it will do specifically for my boss, team, company or the wider community.

Step two: I make sure to engage actively with everyone, most especially those I may not naturally click with. I have a simple method when dealing with those not yet on my Christmas list. Before the start of the meeting or encounter, I find something I really like about the person I connect with the least well. It can even be their smart shoes rather than a personality trait. I focus on that one key positive when I approach them, naturally smiling. It's the principle of positive regard and it works!

It reminds me of when I played competitive rugby; my best teammate was Sarah Escott. Sarah played alongside me at Richmond and for England and we knew that smiling at our enemy unnerved them before we went into battle. We talked about that, we practiced it and we were devilishly good at it!'

Aduke Onafowokan: Champions Everywhere I Look

Aduke Onafowokan's first book is called *The Act of Inclusion*. The title is wonderfully instructive. Inclusion shouldn't just be an idea, a philosophy or an intention. It should be a tangible behaviour at the heart of all smart and thriving communities.

Aduke is a British-Nigerian academic who has worked in and for many male-dominated industries. Her professional journey began in law and IT project management, with roles at Deloitte, British American Tobacco and the UK Ministry of Defence. These experiences as an expert and a leader couldn't help but highlight the challenges faced by women, particularly women of colour, in being welcomed, respected and heard.

I first met Aduke in 2016 as an invitee to a Sister Sister conference she was hosting. I was the only male in a room of 80 attendees and felt welcomed, respected and heard.

The Sister Sister Global Network was Aduke's first venture into social enterprise. In its first decade, it empowered over 12,000 women, and a few male acolytes like me, through leadership and personal development programmes. My relationship with Aduke has been wonderfully reciprocal; she joined, and was a leading light in, our Uspire Leaders' Network in 2018. I pretended I was coaching her when the learning flowed fully my way too.

Aduke's academic background illustrated the breadth of her desire to learn. She has studied at Yale, INSEAD and Oxford University, where she received a Master's in Organisational Leadership. Aduke is a true Captain in the area of diversity, equity and inclusion. She is the founder of a consultancy called Inclusivitii, which is all about helping leaders and their teams act on inclusion. The Sister Sister Global Network has recently rebranded as the Horizon Collective, so please get in contact via the website (https://www.horizoncollective.org) if you are inspired to join the tribe.

Thanks to the Sister Sister Global Network, I have met so many inspiring Captains who have become trusted suppliers and clients. Captains like Bep Dhaliwal (below) as well as Ana Howes, a guru of AI-generated education, and Riffi Khan (mentioned in Chapter 6).

Aduke Onafowokan with Bep Dhaliwal, Captains of positive change in their communities. Photo courtesy of Aduke Onafowokan.

Bep Dhaliwal

I invite you to connect with Bep for the sheer inspiration she brings to every conversation. Her consultancy is called Thrive365 and when you read the list of challenges she has overcome, you'll realise what a remarkable life force she is.

After 20 highly successful years in a corporate career, Bep faced a relentless list of personal challenges. This included divorce, her partner being diagnosed with cancer, and multiple and recurring cancer diagnoses herself:

- Breast cancer in 2013
- Endometrial cancer in 2019
- Bowel cancer in 2023

Bep's coaching on resilience is transformational as she takes a mentoring approach for individuals and teams. In other words, the sharing of her experiences in how best to cope and then to thrive in the most trying and difficult circumstances.

One of my favourite tribes was the brainchild of Ben Grout and Shehla Kadri in East London. Both have been amazing Captains in helping the community in which they live and work.

In 2016 Ben, a financier based in Canary Wharf, enlisted Shehla in an idea to give jobless people in East London a step up to get their first paid employment. Shehla was working for East Thames Housing Association (now known as L&Q Group) which enabled her to seek out candidates for a dedicated mentoring programme.

Her great strength was creating a sense of safety for numerous people who were otherwise anxious of entering a new programme, surrounded by strangers. Many were single parents and most had English as a second language and lacked the confidence to speak it openly.

My role was to be one of the lead facilitators. What made the programme so special was seeing the confidence level change in our delegates after 12 weeks of training, coaching and counselling. We didn't make anything easy for them at the end – because we needed to harden their resolve for the rounds of job interviews. The final step for certification was a *Dragons' Den* style individual presentation to senior executives of HSBC on the 21st floor of the HSBC building. We knew if our delegates could thrive in that environment, they would be well set for any job interview.

2019 team of delegates and educators. Shehla Kadri is on the far right.

Have a watch of this Vimeo clip sharing what that journey felt like: https://vimeo.com/300294065

It is also a fond memory for me of Shehla. She passed away suddenly in 2024 just as she was preparing to launch another amazing project helping those in need. I was part of her delivery team so the news of her passing was particularly devastating for me. It was great to see that Greenwich Council recently dedicated their Housing for Women funding in Shehla's name as a lasting tribute.

The Bottom Line

There are FIVE essentials in establishing a tribe:

1. Recognise the tribe you are in (or go out and form one purposefully).
2. Talk openly about what common goals you have.
3. Seek mentors, allies and diverse perspectives.
4. Find positive regard for all members of the tribe.
5. Embrace winning and failures with exactly the same learning, resilient mindset and compelling passion to change what isn't right.

Capture the key messages that resonated for you in particular in this chapter and note them down in the *OH* column; for each one, put your corresponding intention to act in the *SO* column:

OH	SO

In the next chapter, I'll share how best to get the must-do jobs done by sharing stories about two amazing Captains: one in a government-funded role and the other a chocolate-maker!

Chapter 8

Completer Mentality

This chapter is all about inspiring you to dial up your completer finisher energy.

Christobell Giles

If winning matters for you, ask a chess champion for strategic support; that way, you can align your daily actions (tactics) with your long-term intent (vision). It will help ensure that the outcomes most important for your venture do happen.

Christobell Giles was the Captain of the English chess team before she became a champion of restaurant operations. Her current role is the Managing Director of Vagabond, an exciting concept in wine hospitality where the consumer takes responsibility to explore, pair and self-pour from a wonderfully rich and diverse selection of wines.

With plans to double the size of the business in just three years, Christobell does see a clear correlation between performing in chess and business:

'My superpower is connecting all the dots well in advance so that each move can be purposefully planned. In comparing success in chess and business, here are my three connected essentials:

1. Think several moves ahead.

2. Occupy the centre (emphasise core strengths to bring most leverage).

3. Value each piece with an obsessive focus on developing everyone.'

Spending time with Christobell in the exciting atmosphere of her restaurants reinforces the elements of sporting intelligence: intentionality, tribal spirit, thin-slicing and self-command. You can see each member of the team delivering with a genuine passion for what they do. How can you apply this rigour to your team?

Sandra Colamartino

Sandra Colamartino is one of the best completer finishers I have ever met. In this chapter, she shares how she makes sure she finishes tasks strongly in sport, journalism, theatre production and her own business, Quirky Chocolate. I also share some headlines from her former Scottish teammate, Lisa O'Keefe MBE, who has similar drive and resilience. They both bring big ideas to the table and have combined passion, grit and determination to see projects through to completion.

As the first-ever captain of the Scottish women's rugby team, Sandra Colamartino was also one of the top try scorers in the early years of the team. However, her position as first-choice scrum-half came under threat with the arrival of Paula Chalmers, a natural, supremely talented athlete. It meant that for a few games, Sandra was no longer a first-choice 'starting' player. The rugby term for those who start on the bench is 'finishers', which suited Sandra's character rather well. She would come into the game when the opposition were tiring and gaps for nippy runners like Sandra were appearing more frequently.

Sandra (front row, second from the left) leading Scotland in their first international match against Ireland, 14th February 1993. Photo courtesy of Julie Taylor's mum – who also gave all the team a red rose!

Some of Sandra's big transitions in life were forced upon her; others were of her own making. The end of her rugby career, however, was particularly brutal. In order to fight for her place in the Scotland team, she knew she needed to play rugby at a higher level on a regular basis. With the English league more competitive at that time, she made the courageous decision to persuade her employer (*The Scotsman*) to transfer her to their London office. That meant she could still work for the paper as a graphic designer while playing rugby with the English Champions, Richmond.

Her '*Why not?*' approach to decision-making has made her career journey take multiple twists and turns. Just a few games into the new season in the English premiership, Sandra suffered a catastrophic injury which meant at least a year out from playing. It was a major setback, but one that triggered a fast resetting of goals. Deciding to concentrate 100% on her career at this time, she went on a mission both '*to make myself indispensable*' and to work her way back to Edinburgh.

Her efforts were rewarded when her then-boss, Sue Douglas (the first female editor of a Sunday newspaper, *The Express*), promoted her from graphic designer to magazine editor to head up the launch of the group's new magazine section.

Sandra reflected on this new assignment:

> '*It was highly unusual for a designer to be promoted into an editor's role at that time. Sue could see that a magazine was a much more visual experience compared to a newspaper, so putting someone in place who would prioritise*

the visuals as well as the editorial was a bold decision that certainly ruffled a few feathers! I threw myself into this new role by applying common sense, especially when confronted by highly-experienced journalists. I asked myself: "Does each article keep my attention from the start to the finish? If not, why not? What topics would I like to read about myself? Does this sound interesting to me?" By keeping it simple and not being intimidated by others, I reckon I did a pretty decent job.'

There's a powerful simplicity about Sandra's approach to every challenge: aim high, start fast and make it work, no matter what setbacks you experience. There is an innate boldness strongly connected to the sporting IQ of thin-slicing: have enough information to get going, but don't let too many thoughts stifle your belief, creative thinking and action orientation.

In the spring of 2022, two years before the 30th anniversary of the 1994 World Cup, Sandra felt the event needed to have proper recognition and a reunion of the main participants in the story. She decided that a theatre production would be the best medium to share the story, and set a date for the event to coincide with the exact date 30 years before when Scotland hosted a highly-acclaimed World Cup at short notice.

Herein lies one element of Sandra's secret sauce: when you are breaking new ground, set a completion date and stick to it, no matter what. If you have never written, produced and delivered a play for public consumption before, giving yourself less than two years from idea with no content to the official launch is just bonkers! Sandra says, *'I know that if I had not set a firm deadline, there is no chance the play would ever have happened!'*

A few years after returning to Edinburgh, as newspapers in general faced a downturn, Sandra needed all of her grit and determination to adjust to changing times:

> *'The next job opportunity was as the art director for Condé Nast, based in London. By now, I had met someone and made my life in Scotland. My solution was to persuade my new employer that I could do the job in three long days a week, instead of Monday to Friday, so I could commute to London from Scotland, rather than be based down south. They agreed, so long as I didn't let on to the rest of the staff. It's amazing what you can do if you put your mind to it!'*

Once again, being proactive and bold got Sandra a permanent job back in Scotland in what was to be her last corporate role. She researched every Scottish-based magazine and decided the one she wanted to work for the most was a lifestyle magazine called *Homes & Interiors Scotland*. She took a direct approach, writing to them with her thoughts on what she liked about the magazine and what she would change if she was editor. Sure enough, with pure manifesting as her influencing tool, fate played its part. A few months later, she received a job offer as editor because a vacancy had just arisen. Sandra made the changes she promised in her new role, and the publication won Scottish Magazine of the Year during her time in charge.

In her own words, the best part was *'working alongside and being inspired by two entrepreneurs, David Riddle and Ian McEwan, who first gave me the idea of starting my own business.'* Sandra credits them with giving her the courage to launch her own company in a totally different business sector: that of speciality chocolate.

She picks up the story:

> *'Formed in 2008, Quirky Chocolate has gone through several major iterations to survive. I first started designing just the packaging and buying in the chocolate from another small Scottish supplier. We then had a big hit selling seasonal chocolate directly to consumers and our supplier couldn't keep up with demand. This success allowed us to invest in our own equipment and become chocolate manufacturers. We now have our own factory in Edinburgh where we produce branded products for shops, tourist destinations and premium hotels, as well as consumers.*
>
> *I liken the journey I have been on with Quirky Chocolate like being on a boat on a river. There are times when you try and go upstream and you can do and make ground with sustained effort. Then there are other times, in choppy water, when you're just happy to avoid capsizing and sinking. Through it all, I keep true to my brand's essence: being inclusive and kind, always – to my staff, suppliers, customers and to the environment.*

This year, in order to scale, I've taken on debt for the first time. This is for a special wrapping machine which will enable us to scale significantly. It's another bold step, and one that I've backed up with a lot of research to ensure we know where we are heading as we go upstream.'

Here are Sandra's three suggestions for anyone setting out in their own business:

1. *Set smart goals but don't be too fixed. Throw lots of things at the wall, see what sticks and go all in. If something isn't working, change it quickly and move on.*

2. *Know your core principles against which you should judge everything. This will guide your decision-making.*

3. *Bring eternal optimism to every day at work so that your whole team see it, feed off it and reciprocate it.*

Sandra's tribe at Quirky Chocolate.

Lisa O'Keefe: 'This girl can'

The 20th of December 1994 was the first time the Scotland women's rugby programme (which I was coaching) played two international matches on the same day. We played a first-team and a second-team fixture against Wales concurrently. It was part of our aim to broaden and deepen the talent pool of players we could choose from.

The day was particularly special for Lisa O'Keefe because, rather uniquely, she got to play in both fixtures, including her first full cap for Scotland. Lisa had been close to selection for the 1st XV and would have been the first-team reserve had we not been playing two games. I decided it would be better for her to play and lead the second team rather than keep the bench warm for the firsts!

Both fixtures were attritional and incredibly close, largely driven by the torrential rain that continued throughout the matches. At half-time in the first-team game, Scotland had a narrow lead of just 5–0, thanks to a brilliant solo try from Sandra. We knew that strong reinforcements for the second period would be key if we were to hold on to our first-ever win against the more experienced Welsh team. I called our second-team coach and asked for Lisa to leave her match and come over to be a potential finisher for us.

With five minutes remaining in the first-team match, Wales were camped on the Scotland defence line, pressing for an equalising score. I turned to Lisa on the substitutes bench to enter the game to make a difference and help get us over the line. We hung on for the narrowest of wins, 5–0, and heard that our second team had won by the same close score! I told Lisa that she may be the only sportsperson in history to win two international rugby matches on the same day!

I also shared this wonderful story of Brian Clough, the famous football manager who once read out a team sheet and declared to his Captain, Larry Lloyd, 'Well done for winning two caps for England last week on the same day, Larry; your first and your last!'

In total, Lisa won 45 caps for Scotland between 1994 and 2006, and has since embarked on a groundbreaking career in sports administration, progressing quickly to become a highly successful Director of Sport at Sport England.

Ironically, it was when she moved into the non-budget-holding role of Director of Insight that she was able to create an even bigger impact. Using data and thorough research to inform every strategic decision, the insight team recognised that the solution lay in fixing the system, not the women. Traditional methods of encouraging girls and women to be more active (such as investing in more facilities) weren't creating a step change in the activity levels of women and girls in England.

Instead, the Insight team at Sport England identified the impact of emotional barriers to being active. Further analysis led to the breakthrough insight that a fear of judgement was holding back many women and girls from being more active. This insight inspired the decision to launch a campaign called 'This Girl Can'. It was an instant hit because it spoke directly to its target audience of women and girls about their experiences, in a tone of voice that was empowering, inclusive and humorous, using real and relatable women in the adverts.

Take a moment to analyse this list of barriers to being more active, connected to the fear of judgement. Jot down which one(s) resonate most for you.

- A lack of aptitude for the activity
- Not 'fitting in' with current participants
- Not knowing what is expected
- Not understanding the best way to get going
- Fear of being judged for taking time out for myself

From the insight about fear of being judged, the campaign created some key measures with regard to its impact on women: awareness of the campaign, attitudes towards sport, physical activity and specific actions taken.

The campaign had three key objectives:

- Increase the number of girls and women taking part in sport and physical activity.
- Change how they feel and think about exercising and playing sport.
- Change the opportunities available to women to become active.

To understand how women were feeling and thinking about being active, they tracked three aspects of attitude:

- **Concern:** the degree to which women interviewed agreed that *'I don't worry about what others think of me when exercising.'*

- **Confidence:** the degree to which women interviewed agreed that *'I feel comfortable in myself when exercising.'*

- **Belonging:** the degree to which women interviewed agreed that *'People like me are exercising.'*

Lisa and her team measured these over time and focused on the extent to which the indicators moved as they tried different campaign executions and activations. The 'This Girl Can' campaign had an astonishing and lasting impact, and celebrated 10 years and counting in 2025! One of its notable achievements was to help millions of girls and women think, *'I'm not the only one who feels that way; right, OK then, let's give it a go!'*

I asked Lisa why she felt the campaign resonated so emphatically:

> *'The stars were definitely aligned in that moment. We needed a campaign to kick-start the whole initiative and our CEO at Sport England, Jennie Price, brought expertise in the use of campaigns alongside more traditional investment in infrastructure and engagement programmes. We had a female Secretary of State for Culture and Sport in Dame Maria Miller, and a female Sports Minister in Helen Grant, all backing us fully, and a Sport England Board*

prepared to make insight-led decisions resulting in innovative solutions.

Investing in a robust and independent evaluation enabled us to not only learn and adapt, but also to share learning and demonstrate impact. This was essential in our conversations with the providers of sport and physical activity, who worked with us to adapt provision to better meet the needs of specific target audiences.'

Key metrics included:

- Activity levels of women in England aged 14–40 (changed to 14–60 in later phases)
- Changes in attitude towards being active
- Reach and impact of campaign channels
- Return on investment
- Partner engagement

In the first seven months of Phase One, the campaign achieved over 95 million online views, acquired over 580,000 followers across all platforms and generated online conversations in over 110 countries. In terms of activity levels, 2.8 million women in England aged 14–40 were more active as a result of seeing the campaign, of which 1.6 million started or returned to exercise.

Lisa's current role, on a four-year cycle, is Secretary General for the International Working Group (IWG) on Women & Sport. I asked her how she aims to create as big an impact as possible on this global programme. She said:

'I have three top tips for anyone embarking on trying to win the hearts and minds of multiple stakeholder groups:

1. Stay in tune with the core mission by using research to shape your thinking and make the case.

2. Stay grounded and self-challenging, especially when you have momentum.

3. Create an environment which inspires and empowers others to drive change.'

Photo: Lisa O'Keefe, Secretary General of the IWG.
Photo courtesy of the IWG.

The Completer Finisher

In my life as an independent consultant, I have actively sought out the authors of leadership and business-learning theories. I like to get in-person endorsement of the content I will subsequently and gainfully pass on to my clients. It's not so much about 'stealing with pride' as about knowing their philosophy well enough to be able to share it simply and understandably.

I attended a lecture by the late Dr R. Meredith Belbin at Henley Management College in the days when you couldn't access such speeches on the internet. He was talking about the nine team roles he believes to be essential (in teams or groups) for them to perform and deliver excellently.

During the lunch break, I managed to sit opposite the great man and tried to make engaging chit-chatty conversation whilst the two of us were eating:

'Dr Belbin, your family name is unusual; there can't be too many Belbins in the directory!'

'Indeed,' he replied, glancing over the rim of his glasses, *'In fact, I am the only one.'*

My retort was out of my lips before I had the chance to self-regulate: *'Apart from your mum and dad, of course!'*

The lack of reaction seemed to indicate he was perplexed and not amused!

Here are the nine team roles with my interpretation of the part each plays for a team:

Role Name	Role Descriptor	Example
Plant	The Idea Maker: thinks outside the box	*'Let's think of a different way to approach this.'*
Resource Investigator	The Networker	*'Here's an idea I learnt from another team.'*
Coordinator	The Leader	*'Let's hear everyone's thoughts first.'*
Shaper	The Driver	*'We've talked enough, let's take action.'*
Monitor Evaluator	The Thinker	*'Let's weigh pros and cons before deciding.'*
Team Worker	The Supporter	*'Let's make sure everyone feels heard.'*
Implementer	The Doer	*'Here's a to-do list to make it happen.'*
Completer Finisher	The Finisher	*'Let me double check it before we send it.'*
Specialist	The Expert	*'Let me explain exactly how this works.'*

Even if you have a good understanding of Belbin's team roles, take this moment to reflect on which two or three best reflect your natural behaviours when you are in a team. Are you more of the solution finder, galvanizer of the team or a relentless get-it-done type? The key is to know both what you bring and what other traits you need to surround yourself with to make everything work. Jot down your answers in your notebook.

The vision you started with as a Captain needs to be seen through to the conclusion and finalised with the highest attention to detail and quality. The two Captains mentioned in this chapter have taken what they learnt on the sports field and used the same instincts and self-belief into their careers **beyond** playing.

Belbin describes the 'Completer Finisher' as someone who focuses on quality, brings a sense of urgency and commitment, and meets deadlines with precision. What Sandra has done smartly in Quirky Chocolate is gather a team of 12 permanent staff who bring a passion for chocolate and team spirit as a foundation, and who between them fulfil all of the Belbin team roles. For Lisa, in a role sponsored by governments, success means sourcing the right project team members from a diverse stakeholder group, most of whom are not in the Sport England or IWG setup. They might be from a leisure centre, a sports clothing manufacturer or indeed from a governmental department.

Great Captains surround themselves with a diverse set of talents who embrace the mission as passionately as the Captain does herself.

The Bottom Line

It doesn't matter which field you chose to inhabit once your time as an active player is over. What matters is deciding what you are truly passionate about and finding a way to get actively involved in improving all aspects of it. As the Captain of positive change in your chosen sphere, set yourself tough targets and aspirations, get going fast, be bold and stay on course until the job is complete. Be obsessive about your mission so that you have a profound effect on others who share your ambition. The very best Captains create a lasting legacy and that can be you.

From the insights within this chapter, what are your main takeaways and intentions which resonate with you the most? Write down a decisive action you are going to take for each intention.

OH	SO

In the next chapter, *Making Connections*, I share three must-use tools to find and influence the right people to enable your Captaincy aspirations to be achieved and take flight.

Chapter 9

Making Connections

This chapter is packed with easy-to-use tools to help you influence key decisions which are vital for the success of your Captaincy. Many of these will challenge your current methods of persuasion. I share thought-provokers as well as planning tools. In addition, there are three stories about truly inspiring people who not only make strong connections easily, but also exhibit the key influencing skills I'll share.

To persuade, the 'dolphin trainer' principle from Chapter 6 applies throughout; **establish trust first**.

For the last 25 years, I have led learning companies which design and deliver educational events in the corporate world. I have created and pressure-tested what I am about to share in terms of how to connect deeply and quickly with all sorts of people, especially the ones who are wired differently to you. Those wired differently to you are often key to making your dreams a tangible reality.

Thought Provocation Number 1

We need a whole new approach to cut through the noise.

Let's challenge the old adage that *'It's not what you know, it's who you know'*. In my experience, connection with the right people is all about translating your message into their language (their brain wiring). It means that persuading people to achieve the positive outcomes you desire is absolutely about **what you know** and how well you select the appropriate elements of that knowledge to share with **who you know**. The skills of dynamic interaction are central. The story of connections I'll share next is to encourage you to grab all opportunities that arise.

Luke Melnik

Here's a story of a series of wholly diverse connections which ended up with me working in ice hockey for the first time, a sport I have absolutely no background in. And yet I now coach a brilliant young Canadian ice hockey player called Luke Melnik. He wants to be a star one day in the National Hockey League in North America. His dad, Patrick, is an acquaintance of Colombian entrepreneur Simone Fernandez. I worked for Simone in Sao Paolo over a three-year period and during our time together, I shared my background in sports psychology with her, which she evidently shared with Patrick in a casual conversation some years later.

My introduction into mental coaching came when my Swedish client Mikael Hagman (whom I met when we attended a leadership programme together at Henley Management College) asked me in 2006 to help his beloved football team AIK Stockholm get their psychology sorted out to win something again. As the best supported club in Sweden, Mikael told me that AIK had not won anything since the turn of the century and that it was a situation he needed to solve quickly.

When AIK subsequently won the Allsvenskan in 2009 (the All-Sweden Championship), my reputation for making an impact in the mental side of sport was established. It was rather cool being called 'Dr Gold' by the fans and local press! If I had not met Mikael, I would not have established credibility as a mental coach. Without that experience, Simone would not have recommended me to Patrick, Luke's dad, more than a decade later.

In my first meeting with Luke, I introduced him to the principles of SpQ and the T.E.A.R. model. I reflected after the meeting with Luke about what an amazing set of connections these are that brought me to sharing content in a specific meeting with a young Canadian athlete.

Thought Provocation Number 2

When presenting your ideas, don't think about the content first.

It's a natural thing to do. Someone asks you to present and so you grab your laptop and start creating content-rich slides. Instead, use the A.B.C.D. method (see page 41) to deliver a totally audience-relevant presentation.

Thought Provocation Number 3

One brilliant question can change the other person's brain pattern.

The biggest skill gap I witness when I observe conversations in a business setting is the combination of poor questioning and only selective listening. This is usually due to a pre-conceived view of what the answer should be, often from both sides. This is especially true if one party is trying to sell a product or service; if the focus is to sell, it usually isn't to listen and learn.

The skill I train that has the biggest immediate impact on every audience who hear it for the first time is **'high-gain'** questions. A high-gain question is a strategic, open-ended question that is intended to draw out the most valuable, detailed information from someone as efficiently as possible. It is truly transformational to use a high-gain question in any important conversation. This is because it forces the other person to reflect, analyse and compare before they give the answer. That guarantees that the answer you receive has more thought-through substance and value (often for both parties).

How do you create a high-gain question?

First, be clear what key information you would like to gather. Then, start with an open question such as 'What do you need?' and insert one or two **keywords** to elevate it. That way, it becomes more targeted. For example:

*'What **exactly** do you need?'* or
*'What are your **top** three needs now?'*

| Be clear what **INFORMATION** you need | **INSERT** key words into an open question | Words which force reflection, comparison & decision |

Here are some more **inserted** word high-gain question examples:

What's your **biggest** challenge?
If budget was not an issue, what **specifically** would you do?
What are your **top 3** aims?
What does **perfect** look like in your eyes?
What worked **best**?
Describe the implications **in detail**
What **exactly** are you looking for?

I was a trainee on a workshop run in Dublin by the world-class educator Tony Griffin, a Captain helping Irish teenagers find their purpose and mojo. (Look up the amazing Soar organisation in Ireland, which Tony founded, https://www.soar.ie). He asked each member of the learning group I was part of to mention one superpower that they possessed. When my turn came, I said, *'Asking high-gain questions.'*

Tony replied in an instant,

> *'Great! I'd like everyone to prove the value of these questions. Please go outside now onto the streets of Dublin and ask the first person you see a high-gain question. You have 30 minutes and be ready to report back what happened.'*

The Captaincy

I am normally an activist learner but with this task, I was unusually nervous, thinking how to soften asking a big question to a complete stranger. Fortunately, I met a kind, mature man wearing a fun, green bobble hat with the word 'Dublin' emblazoned on it.

Ted in his 'Dublin' bobble hat!

'I like your hat,' I said, by way of introduction. *'It looks like you might be a local yourself.'*

When he confirmed that indeed he was a Dubliner, I continued with my high-gain question: *'Which three aspects of this amazing city stand out for you?'*

His answer, which took some time to formulate, sparked a deep 30-minute conversation which made me late for Tony's stated return time! Ted said,

> *'I reckon Dublin is special because of the people, the craic and Saturday morning walks in town with my nine-year-old granddaughter.'*

Naturally, I asked him to explain more about each of those and we discussed some deeply personal aspects of his life, all triggered by one high-gain question.

Take a moment now to choose a high-gain question you intend to ask in your very next meeting and jot it down. When you use it, see how it makes your audience look reflective and intrigued.

Thought Provocation Number 4

Decision-makers can be influenced by someone other than you.

This tool is called a Stakeholder Decision Map. It helps clarify how to navigate the decision-making process, beyond just the perceived decision-maker alone.

For each of the major decisions you are looking to influence, there will be a number of people you have a vested interest (stake) in the outcome. The photo below is me with Zimbabwean Tawanda Matanda at a workshop in Thailand. Tawanda is a key stakeholder for my work with the United Nations, and the photo depicts how important the stake is!

Me in one of my 'Zoom shirts' with Tawanda Matanda, sharing stories about our amazing mums.

In the following image, I have simplified these stakeholders into three key categories: decision-makers, key influencers and users (those impacted by the decision with little or no influence on it). Draw this image in your notebook and list each stakeholder connected to your proposal. Then decided which stakeholder goes into which category. Next, decide if each one is either a supporter of your proposal, a critic and opposed to the idea, or if they are sitting neutrally on the fence.

Notice how I have combined the three types of stakeholder with their three possible perspectives. It means that once you have plotted all the stakeholders, you will have a clear visual representation (map) of how you (or one of the supporters) might go about influencing the decision outcome. This means that you can now write your step-by-step influencing plan.

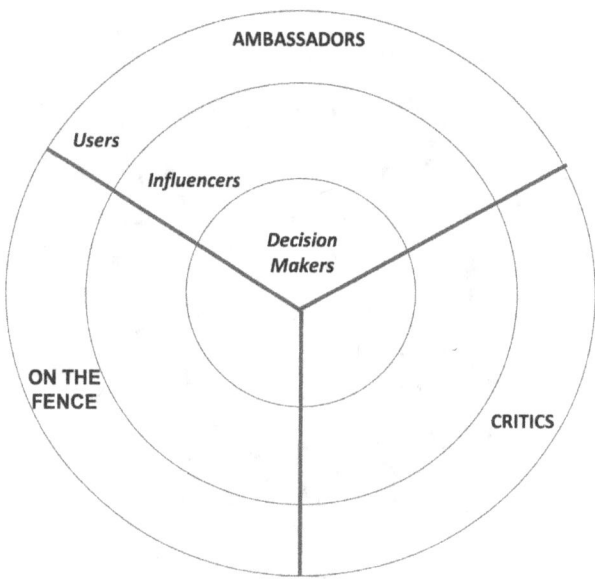

Thought Provocation Number 5

One ordinary person with resolve CAN change government policy.

I actively find ways to spend time amongst the Captains I highlight in this book. They have an aura connected both to who and how they are, not just for what they have achieved. Pam Warren is a prime example. She is pure inspiration for me whether I am with her in person or online.

Pam Warren

Pam's book *From Behind the Mask* is a bestseller that continues to sell in huge numbers more than 25 years after the incident which inspired it and transformed Pam's life forever. Pam's book is the only book I have ever read three times. It details her harrowing journey from trauma to empowerment. Each time I read it, I notice a different aspect of her character and her impact through her remarkable storytelling skills.

Here's Pam Warren on our Boostcast podcast at the height of the pandemic in 2020. Photo courtesy of Pam Warren.

Pam was a successful financial planner in the City of London when she boarded a train from Reading to the capital on the morning of 5th October 1999. On that fateful journey, the train collided with another on the tracks at Ladbroke Grove, just outside Paddington. Thirty-one people lost their lives and more than 500 were injured. In the moment, Pam remembers thinking, *'If this is it for me, has it all been worth it?'*

A fireball ripped through the Pam's carriage and she suffered burns to her hands and face, and such extensive lung damage that the first responders concluded *'No hoper'* in the triage notes. Pam was taken to hospital and was in a coma for three months.

On the long, arduous and brutally painful road to recovery, Pam had more than 23 reconstructive surgeries and was required to wear a clear Perspex® mask to protect the recently-grafted new facial skin. The mask became a haunting symbol of pain, resilience and survival that would later become a powerful emblem of her advocacy for systemic improvements to the British rail network.

Being a campaigner had never been in Pam's plans when she first attended a Paddington survivors' gathering some months after the accident. The more time passed, the more she realised that no meaningful change to rail safety would happen without an organised, properly-led campaign to highlight the must-fix issues. She co-founded the Paddington Survivors' Group and became a vocal critic of the UK rail industry's complacency.

Pam became a Captain driving all related parties towards taking tangible responsibility for improvement in rail safety. At one point when all momentum for change seemed to have ceased, the then Transport Minister, Stephen Byers, gave updates on discussions he had held with the Survivors' Group. Such was Pam's influence by then that she used the media to call out a significant lie in his statement. This was one of the reasons Byers had to resign from the government for what was described euphemistically as *'misleading parliament'*[8].

Pam's efforts were not born out of ambition, but necessity; to make sure that the tragedy she endured would never be repeated. Her work led to several investigations (in other rail disasters as well) and changes in railway management and policy. This included the phased removal of older signal systems that had contributed to the Paddington crash.

In the years since the accident, Pam has transformed herself into a much sought-after speaker, author and advocate for change. She is also a blooming good gardener if her wonderful Welsh home and grounds are anything to go by! In well-earned semi-retirement she still speaks not only about rail safety, but also about overcoming adversity, building mental resilience, and the importance of changing pain into purpose. It's a fable on how to turn tragedy into growth by force of will and the ability to say the right things to the right people, in order to drive lasting change.

Pam's success as an influencer is based on tireless research, raw honesty and a lawyer's attention to the

---

[8] http://news.bbc.co.uk/1/hi/uk_politics/2013061.stm

details that all solutions to change require. When I asked her to join two Boostcasts I was hosting during Covid, her probing questions were all high-gain (of course!).

Thought Provocation Number 6

You don't have to be loud to be a great Captain.

Carol Isherwood

Carol Isherwood OBE was the first Chair of the Women's Rugby Football Union in 1985, the first Great Britain Captain, the first England Women's Captain **and** a Club Captain I had the pleasure to work alongside at Richmond. In addition, she has just become the first Chair of the Women's British and Irish Lions'. Her gift to sport has always been to grow participation exponentially. She has done so with simple pragmatism alongside a much-needed political canniness. She is a Captain of making connections.

Carol Isherwood – a Captain for the advancement of rugby and football globally.

When she became the first Chair of the fledgling Women's Rugby Football Union, she approached all the universities playing women's rugby. She advised that when players graduated, they should go back home to their local men's clubs and promise that if the club let them play women's matches on Sunday afternoons, the bar takings would go up dramatically! In the first three years of her tenure, the number of active women's rugby clubs rose from a handful to over 70. It was by some way the fastest growing sport in Britain in the 1990s.

Carol has much to answer for in my life! Without her convincing her Leeds University friend, Scottish sprint champion Debbie MacLaren, to take up rugby and then play alongside her for college, club, country, and Great Britain, I wouldn't have met my now-wife of 36 years! My two older boys, Ben and James, would not have grown up thinking rugby was a game for women, or that when they represented Scotland themselves at under-17 and under-19 level, it wasn't as cool as their mum's achievements. Debbie is Scotland's only female British Lioness. Debs played in England's first game because Scotland didn't have a team in 1986. Seven years later, Scotland formed a national team and Debbie was allowed to transfer her playing allegiance!

In the following image, you can see that Debbie is No. 7 on Scotland's Honours Board at Murrayfield, and No. 4 on the England's Honours Board at Twickenham, the home of English Rugby! Carol is No. 6 on that board!

Just to round off how pioneering and influential Carol has been, she was the first woman appointed as a council member of the International Rugby Board in 2011 and one of the first female inductees into the World Rugby Hall of Fame in 2014. She is still one of the first to start a right good sing-song whenever the clan gathers; *Running Bear* by Johnny Preston being a personal favourite of mine.

See if you can find Carol near the top left at a 30-year reunion of England and Scotland players from the 1994 World Cup. A photograph simply packed with Captains!

Thought Provocation Number 7

Storytelling is a critical skill set
to influence real change.

Donghyuk Park

I first met Donghyuk Park in Geneva at an International Organisation for Migration (IOM) conference that I was facilitating. When Donghyuk spoke, everybody listened intently so I tried to detect what he did specifically to capture attention. By the time we worked together again in Thailand a year later, two things had happened. First, I had realised that his secret sauce was a gift for compelling storytelling. Second, he had just been promoted to the position of Chief of Mission for Guinea. This is the highest UN role in each country.

On his LinkedIn profile, Donghyuk shares how he honed his skills:

> 'Having worked in journalism, I gained valuable professional experience in uncovering compelling stories and then focusing on effectively disseminating them – a skill I learned over time.'

Donghyuk was a policeman in Seoul before he became a journalist in Paris. It's a suitably diverse background which has helped him traverse the challenges of influencing stakeholder groups in his Mission in West Africa. When you are seeking donors to fund your projects, and seeking governmental support from those people who are distracted by a plethora of issues, you need a storyteller's prowess to grab attention and start to influence mindsets and behaviours.

Every educational institution, from the earliest kindergarten, should have storytelling classes alongside maths, reading and writing as the fundamental elements of their curriculum.

A well-crafted and relevant story is the most effective way to connect your message with other people because it links to our emotions as well as our intellect. Good storytelling also changes the listener's physiology by inspiring endorphin release in the body. It is surprising, therefore, that it is almost never taught in schools or as part of an induction to business. It means standard presentations are slide-deck heavy, wordy, and story-less – and, frankly, rather dull!

Nine out of ten presentations I witness start like this:

> 'Hi, um, good morning. For those of you who don't know me, my name is…'

How dull and uninspiring is that?!

However, 100% of TEDx talks start immediately with a story. This is to hook attention and interest (the head and the heart) right from the start. If you want your Captain's message heard and remembered, invest in your storytelling skills.

In his brilliant book, *Seven Stories Every Salesperson Must Tell*, Mike Adams shares how he became a hugely successful influencer just by teaching himself how to use stories to hook, untangle and land his target 'big fish' customers.

C.E.O. Method

I have simplified my training sessions on storytelling to three core steps.

Once you have established the hero of your story, simply follow the **C.E.O. method.**

Give *context*, then share an *event* with related *emotions* and then the *outcome*.

Great stories follow this simple three-step sequence. Here's a true story using the steps:

> '*I was reluctant to write a book because I didn't have a clue how to start. One day, as I sat in my car waiting for the rain to stop, out of the blue my phone rang, and the whirlwind that is Brenda Dempsey quickly created excitement about maybe – just maybe – capturing my thinking in a book. Two weeks later, I started writing!*'

Take a moment now to think of an important topic or message you would like to share. What story would bring that to life in an impactful way? Use the C.E.O. method above and then read the story out loud, as if you were in front of your target audience. The three steps will help you structure your message in a succinct and compelling way.

The Bottom Line

Making powerful connections requires you to be targeted, bold and adaptive. Aim as high as the sky. Be conscious of planning and rehearsing your approach.

You know the routine now at the close of the chapter! Fill in your personal call to action.

OH	SO

In the next chapter, I'll share how important it is to measure progress in any change initiative, and not simply to focus on the final results.

Chapter 10

Measuring Progress

When I started writing this book, I wrote this chapter first. Although I shared my manuscript more dutifully in a proper sequence with my publisher, Brenda Dempsey, I wrote this chapter first because, without measures to judge themselves by, Captains can't be certain they're winning. It should be the first thing you do once you have a clear sense of purpose. I know it comes from my innate red energy – the colour energy that demands task focus and clear, tangible results.

For the 30 years I was a coach at Richmond Women's Rugby Club (1986–2016), I was obsessive about creating a culture of continued success. My fellow coach, Simon Crabb, and I had four core principles to work by and stick to:

- Fittest team
- Purposeful practice
- Improvement obsession
- Team first

Take a moment to consider what are the core principles or markers you would like to see within the team you lead or work with and jot them down in your notebook. Ensure you take a balanced approach – make sure it includes behavioural markers, not just outcome goals.

At Richmond, Simon and I put in place simple measures for each of these principles to ensure we were creating an environment conducive to inclusive high performance. Inclusive high performance meant that even those members in our squads who played rugby for recreational fun would find enjoyment and motivation in being the best possible version of a recreational player in a combat sport. For those people specifically, we monitored engagement with teammates outside match days to ensure those with low competitive energy always felt part of the tribe.

Whenever our first team reached the National Final, we ordered extra buses to take our full membership (around 100) along, so they could cheerlead and share the special experience as one community.

This chapter is about inspiring you to measure the things that really matter on a daily basis in your chosen field, not just the final goal. That's not to say final-outcome goals aren't super important. At Richmond in that 30-year period, we won 31 National and European titles, including four consecutive European Championships. It is a true measure of sustained high achievement. Crucially, throughout those three decades, we focused on key input measures which would enable these impressive results (outputs).

What gets measured and is valued gets done.

Fittest Team

Ross Smitheman was our fitness coach in the early years at Richmond. He was a highly competitive rower and fit as a fiddle himself. He was a relentless, obsessive taskmaster who ran what he called a *'20-minute fitness blast'* at the start of our training every Tuesday and Thursday evening. He measured each player's fitness start point and their session-by-session progress with dedicated precision. He also had countless one-to-ones to motivate each player, with a greater attention to all-round personal growth.

As head coach, I then had four squad-wide checkpoints in each season when we ran a bleep test. Those four measure points were at the start and end of our pre-season training, pre-Christmas and at Easter (before the final crucial trophy-deciding matches). One season, the Easter fitness results were significantly down since the Christmas set. We decided this came more from tiredness than from a slackening in attitude. Put simply, we were overtraining, and as a result, we cut one session a week for a month, just to give the squad more recovery time. The outcome was that we reached that year's championship final fresh and ready.

The bleep test is a common way to measure cardiovascular fitness and aerobic capacity. You run back and forth between two lines that are 20 metres apart. You must reach each line before a beep sounds. The beeps get progressively faster in levels and when you miss two consecutive beeps, it indicates the level you have reached. With a sense of relief and frustration for each athlete, that's when the bleep test ends.

If you are non-sporty, a general average on the test would be to attain Level 6. You can reach that without ever having to sprint fully. If you managed three shuttles (there and back) at the start of the new level before you missed two beeps, your final rating might, for example, be Level 8.3. Those in the military, fire or police service need a minimum standard of Level 9 to be considered fit for duty. When I coached the RAF rugby team for a season, they said Level 10 was the minimum standard; not so easy if you were picked in the squad for power and bulk.

For our recreational players (who mostly played in our third XV), we aimed for Level 7. For our elite athletes in the top teams, Level 9 was a base and Level 13 was the aspiration (that is elite). In our early years, I remember the England men's team had a player who reached Level 18. That means he could still sprint at full pace after more than 20 minutes of increasingly hard running. The first team players at Richmond aimed for Level 14 and three made Level 15 by mid-season. I was super fit at the time and was beaten before Level 14.

Purposeful Practice

The expression *practice makes perfect* is riddled with danger. If you keep practicing the wrong things, you'll simply repeat the mistakes you are currently making when it comes to game time. Simon and I set the intention of making all practice as close to game situations as possible. We would start each session with 20 minutes of intense fitness, so that the drills we did next were when players were more physically tired – akin to being asked to deliver a top performance towards the end of a tight match.

When I work in professional football, my specialism is preparing teams for the end of season play-offs, with a particular focus on excellence in penalties. This is because there is an 18% chance that one of the knock-out games will go to a sudden-death penalty shoot-out. When England had just lost a World Cup game on penalties, the then England Manager, Bobby Robson, famously observed,

> 'We don't practice penalties because you cannot accurately replicate the pressure and tension and exhaustion you have to overcome when taking penalties in a knock-out game situation.'

Bobby was wrong!

The purposeful practice that I have been part of for five successful penalty shoot-outs (I hope I am not tempting fate!) is to first practice only at the end of a hard training session, when the players are physically and mentally tired. Then give them just one chance to score. Set the team up at the halfway line and ask them to make the long walk to the penalty spot – in total silence. One chance only, just like in a shoot-out for real.

When we did this at AFC Wimbledon in 2011, ahead of the Conference League final against Luton Town, we also added squad response to each penalty... so if you missed your penalty, you were mainly shunned by teammates, but if you scored, you were mobbed by everyone. This meant we practiced outcome (consequence) behaviours, as well as the precursory ones. The boys weren't called the 'Crazy Gang' for nothing! We won on penalties 4-3.

When Carlisle United reached the League 1 play-off final at Wembley on 28th May 2023, we had measured every player's success rate under the same elements of pressure-based practice. We practiced relentlessly and purposely for four weeks before the play-offs. This meant that, when we came to penalties against Stockport County, we knew, in player sequence, who within our squad was most certain to score at the moment of highest pressure. We also knew which of the three senior goalkeepers was the best shot-stopper for penalties.

I had added a small tweak to the practice around breathing more deeply and smiling on the long, lonely walk from the halfway line. It can be especially eerie in a stadium when 60,000 people are hushed! When the moment came for Taylor Charters to take the decisive penalty at Wembley, he broke all the conventions and jogged quickly to the penalty spot, laughing visibly and joyously.

At Richmond, we had two simple ways to sense-check that our practices were purposeful. How tired did our fittest players look at the end of the session? If they didn't have their hands on their knees, sucking in extra oxygen, we had made the practice too routine and not enough like the stress in match conditions. We also monitored communication levels; was what we were seeing and hearing game-relevant, or just social catch-up chit-chat? If it was chit-chatty, we weren't practicing with enough intensity.

Me with Paul Simpson, who masterminded the penalty shoot-out win, with conscious use of SpQ.

One of the consistent push-backs I get running training sessions in business from participants is, *'Please don't make us do role plays; we hate them!'* Once again, just practice itself doesn't make perfect. Business simulations need to be as close to the real job as you can make them. For example, when I work with multilingual groups, I insist they practice in the language they usually use at work, even when the input from me is in English. It means the practice is purposeful.

Improvement Obsession

Great Captains are obsessed with seeing proper progression. At Richmond, I established a routine of writing feedback for every player straight after every game. I would highlight their greatest strength and one area to focus on next time. As soon as each game finished, I would start writing 23 feedback sheets! When the players gathered post-shower, we had a team debrief and then I would give each player their personalised feedback. This ensured that not only did individuals improve, but also the collective impact became observable too.

It is lovely when I meet up with former players like Scottish international Jeni Sheerin – now a successful business owner and mother to three talented daughters – and they tell me they still have those feedback notes I gave them.

Team First

At one stage at Richmond, we were undefeated for an entire calendar year. It really is an amazing feeling in elite sport to feel invincible. We had attracted the Captains of New Zealand, Italy, Sweden, Spain, Holland, England, Scotland and Wales into our playing squads, which made winning a whole lot easier. The dangers are, of course, the potential of too many leaders. The solution right from the first pre-season session was to create open dialogue and player-led behavioural contracting. From that point, the core measure is simply the level and quality of communication, especially between Captains.

In 30 years, 318 players played for Richmond's first team, 40% of whom were to become full internationals. We won 586 matches – 80% of those we played – with an average game score of 31-7. The wider club played 1,445 matches with a win record of 73% (our second

Richmond uniquely fielded three senior team squads for 15 consecutive years.

XV and third teams were largely playing against first XVs). We created the largest playing squad in the world, involved in more matches, winning more games and scoring more points than any other rugby club. Of all these numbers and statistics, I am most proud of the number of Captains beyond sport that this dynasty produced, many of whom are highlighted in these pages.

Shannon Winzer: Measuring Progress as a Solo Athlete

One of my favourite coaches to try and emulate is Canadian Shannon Winzer, especially her ways of establishing and maintaining high-performance cultures. She is Head Coach of the Canadian National women's volleyball team.

I admire Winzer's Captaincy because:

1. She balances being a be-there Mum and a high-performance coach, which sets a great precedent for future female coaches.
2. She masters holistic athlete development.

3. She has created a behavioural observation system which drives a winning culture.

When Winzer transferred from head coach in Australia to Canada, she discovered a culture that was sorely in need of a revamp. She implemented 'behavioural tracking' against the cultural principles she knew were paramount to any transformation. Poignantly, she believes that:

> *'Culture isn't what we say we value; it's what we actually do. By tracking specific squad behaviours, we could see our real culture rather than our aspirational one.'*

The tracking system included:

- Defined and shared behavioural markers for each cultural principle.
- Regular, formal observation focused exclusively on the markers.
- Documented analysis trends and the correlation to performance outcomes.

For example, while team members were reporting valuing selflessness in surveys, behavioural observation revealed a significant increase in frustration with teammates when mistakes were made. This insight enabled Winzer to specify the changes she expected.

When I translated this idea into the client projects I run, it was transformational. One example is in the hospitality industry, where the Guest Experience teams were jumping straight from the Welcome to explaining what would happen next. They were missing the crucial discovery step to find out what expectations the guests have for their experience. Knowing this (by asking curious questions) enables the host to adapt the experience provided to be certain it meets or exceeds those expectations.

We implemented a 'behavioural tracking system', which first asked for a minimum of three open questions before any experiential storytelling. Initially, we were just tracking quantitatively, so it was yes or no against the three-question target. Over time, we have evolved the tracking to measure the quality of those questions as well.

Here is the moment of greeting in a winery in Australia's Barossa Valley. After the Welcome, these three valuable open questions could be tracked:

- What brings you here today?
- What are you most hoping for in the tasting?
- What special occasions could you be planning for with your wine choices today?

Observational tracking is the best way to discover whether the behaviours which work best are being exhibited and honed. It is also the way to give fact-based feedback to employees who are eager to learn, improve and succeed.

Some of my clients are sceptical of the connection between training and improved results: *'You can't really say that it was the training which helped to produce the stronger sales results.'* One way to prove the point is to measure the performance of those who were trained, tracked and coached against staff yet to be trained. In one English winery, sales were up 45% year-on-year in 2025 in what is a relatively static market. Is all of that down to plain good fortune? I think not!

That's why behavioural tracking is key, especially when connected to guest survey scores.

Who Should Do the Measuring?

Create a feedback culture whereby everyone feels a degree of ownership for behavioural excellence. In that way, self-assessment and correction becomes the norm.

In my time working as an assistant coach in football, I have worked with a number of different managers. Mikael Stahre from Sweden is one of my favourite coaches to work with because he believes that players should self-regulate. He sets the standards, gets engagement and endorsement from the players for these standards, and then expects them to manage the implementation.

One example when we were working together at AIK Stockholm was that no mobile phones were allowed to be used in the changing room before the game. They could only be turned on when players walked back into the changing room once the game was over.

On one occasion in 2006, when Micke was an assistant coach, the Swedish international colossus Johan Mjällby walked into the changing room talking loudly on his Blackberry Pearl mobile phone. He was met with jeers and tuts from his teammates and he quickly switched it off. Micke noted that effect of a self-regulating team and when he became head coach, he created a winning culture that saw AIK become National League Champions in 2009.

Be a Captain Long Before You Are a Captain

There are two must-read books on the topic of establishing a culture of sporting excellence: *Legacy* by James Kerr and *Wolfpack* by Abby Wambach.

James Kerr's *Legacy* tells the story of how New Zealand rugby set the tone of behaviour long before players join the set-up. It's a culture that asks all players, including the most senior, to 'sweep the sheds' after playing. It is a culture of personal responsibility and humility which remains long after each era of players have moved on. The principle is that each new international is a custodian of the jersey for a short time, and must treasure it and add value to it beyond simply playing the game. The intention is to leave it in a better place than when he first put it on.

The New Zealand team management monitor discretionary effort and intrinsic motivation. Kerr adds, *'We identify leadership behaviours in individuals long before we assign leadership titles.'*

Wolfpack is a compact, empowering read about how the USA women's soccer team established a winning dynasty. Wambach says, *'The power of the wolf is the pack and the power of the pack is the wolf.'*

She sets a philosophy which should inspire Captains everywhere to shake off convention and embrace change courageously.

Using Wambach's philosophy, here are my suggestions on some custom metrics by which to choose your job and organisation:

- My contributions are recognised, regardless of my title or background.
- I see women in visible leadership roles.
- I am encouraged to challenge the status quo.
- I feel empowered to lead in every role.
- Diversity is wholeheartedly embraced.

One of the initiatives I am proud to support is WISH (Women in Sport High-Performance Pathway programme), run by the University of Hertfordshire in partnership with the International Olympic Committee (IOC). It is a 21-month development opportunity for all female coaches hoping to make an impact at Olympic level.

Since its inception, WISH has engaged 125 women coaches across 22 sports from 60 countries, with 120 graduates completing the programme. Carol Isherwood (see Chapter 9), one of the WISH mentors, invited me to be on the coaching of coaches list, ahead of the Paris Olympic Games. This was an easy project to measure, because in Paris there were 13 coaches who were alumni of the programme. One, Cécile Landi, coached American gymnast Simone Biles to three gold medals, and another, Suvi Mikkonen, a Finnish coach, guided Hungary's Viviana Márton to a gold medal in taekwondo.

The number of female coaches in Paris was 25% of the total, double those of the Tokyo Olympics in 2020. We see that statistic both as a sign of progress and a remaining challenge.

Lini Kazim is now head of Triathlon Development for all of Asia.

My coachee in the WISH programme is the brilliant Malaysian triathlon coach Lini Hayati Binti Nik Kazim (I call her Lini). One of her challenges as a coach in Malaysia, and indeed across Asia, is trying to measure progress when her top athletes might not reach the qualifying criteria to make it to the Olympic Games. If you aren't at the top table, then how do you measure? As her work is foundational, her strategy is to develop many more coaches to cover the whole of the country, and make sure no talent is missed. This is an input measure aiming for more Olympic-qualified Asian triathletes for Los Angeles in 2028.

The Captaincy

Set Targets Connected to Performance, Not Just Results

I had the great pleasure to work with swimmer Eleanor Broughton, when she was preparing for the British Swimming Championships in her last year at Repton School. She was concerned that her best time would place her sixth in the pending national final. We talked about the T.E.A.R. model and changing her focus from watching the clock to loving the challenge. Eleanor texted me the result soon after it happened, just to reinforce the point!

Eleanor is now swimming competitively in the US collegiate system which sets the global standard for elite swimmers.

Eleanor Broughton wins the national championship by two tenths of a second! Photo courtesy of David Broughton.

The Bottom Line

Once you have decided what you wish to Captain, set the principles by which you will make all key decisions. Then establish non-negotiable standards of behaviour (ideally through collaboration with the team themselves) which will be monitored, measured and rewarded for progress and end results. In that way, you create a high-performance environment which can drive and sustain success.

Here's the *Oh! And So?* moment to capture your intent now:

OH	SO

In the final chapter, I'll share who I see as the best leader the world has seen in the last 70 years and two other global-change Captains (for equality and peace). All three stood under 165 centimetres tall. Can you guess who they might be?

Chapter 11

Taking Action!

You are one decision away from a completely different life! Every single revolution, every breakthrough, every lasting legacy, began not with a multipurpose master plan, but with a moment of action. Above all and no matter what, this chapter will inspire you to choose Captaincy. The people I mention are all activists in their chosen passions, with one exception – someone who was not the slightest bit activist by design. And yet her impact was life-improving across the globe for generations of people.

In this chapter, look out for a King, a Queen, a Martyr and a Clown!

At least three of the players I had the privilege to coach at Richmond Rugby Club are now professional film-makers. Their work inspires us to be better.

In 2024, Victoria Rush made her directorial debut with the documentary, *No Woman, No Try* (available on Amazon Prime). The inspiration came from her work as founder of the grassroots empowerment campaign #IAmEnough. Her goal was to reach decision-makers and mainstream audiences, not just athletes. Her core message has landed with parents and their aspiring children alike. Here she is:

No Woman, No Try addresses gender bias in rugby, and highlights issues such as access, funding, visibility and societal expectations around women in sport. When I was the Chair of the Women's Premiership Group from 2013 to 2016, the English Rugby Union were investing £64 million a year into grassroots men's rugby and yet the budget allocated to the elite women's club competition was just £1.5m (which is 2% of the men's). Funding was, and still is, institutionally skewed towards male sport.

Rather fittingly, Victoria made a significant impact in the media coverage of the 2025 Women's Rugby World Cup (held in the UK), just like her predecessor and now film-maker Alice Cooper, who was Head of Media for the inaugural World Championship in Cardiff in 1991.

'We've Run Out of Milk'

I am not a woman. I cannot begin to know what it's like to be treated as second class. I am a white, privately educated, six-foot-four man, carrying the discomforting moniker 'privileged' for more than 60 years.

I am not black. I cannot begin to imagine what it's like to arrive at a major conference as the honorary guest speaker and be approached at the coffee machine by a young besuited white man and be asked to fetch a refill of milk.

For this to be a regular occurrence in any person's life is shameful. To be able to brush it off maturely because there's a better way to influence change than to blurt out with defiance, is a sign of mature, resilient calmness. Here's a handy mantra for all Captains, like Dr Mena Fombo:

- Believe in better
- Others before me
- I am Captain

Mena Fombo

> *'My career is testimony to the principle that it's better to be a jack of all trades than a master of one.'*

Mena Fombo has always been a ceaseless source of positive energy and spontaneous joy ever since I first met her as a promising player at Richmond Rugby

*Mena Fombo at the BAFTA Awards in 2024.
Photo courtesy of Mena Fombo.*

Club. She was both a presence and a force as an athlete and remains so in what she describes as her 'portfolio career'. She is a founder, facilitator and film-maker who impacts key projects across England's South West, such as youth development in her community. She harbours big ambitions to reach and inspire as many people of all ages as possible to big themselves up. She says,

> 'I have taken my inspiration from my grandmother who told me from a young age in her Opobo-dialect of Nigerian, "All my children, whether they are boys or girls, will have the opportunity to travel and to do whatever they want to do."'

Mena shared the lessons she learnt in sport which she now uses in her various projects:

'There were more mentors on the way, of course. I took my view on how to lead from two of my sports coaches: you and Brian, our coach at the Birmingham Lions. In both cases, we were pretty dominant on the field but the key element of success was a culture where you as leaders paid attention to everybody, noticed everybody, and made sure each and every contribution was noticed, called out and recorded.'

Mena is an Ambassador for the City of Bristol (helping more than 9,000 people find accommodation), has an honorary doctorate from the University of West England, runs a successful film company called Blak Wave Productions (helping over 150 freelancers over the last five years) and is a brilliant conference speaker on inclusion and equality.

One thing she passionately wants to exclude is people touching her hair. She started a campaign in 2017 called, *'No. You cannot touch my hair!'* to highlight that certain behaviours aren't acceptable with complete strangers. *'If I was male, would you be touching my hair unannounced?'*

The campaign was so successful in terms of millions of social media impressions that Mena was invited to host a TED Talk on the subject: www.ted.com/talks/mena_fombo_no_you_cannot_touch_my_hair_jun_2023

The Three Greatest Captains I Have Never Met!

Malala Yousafzai

Malala Yousafzai fell in love with school partly because her father ran a girls' school in her village in Swat Valley, Pakistan. Everything changed for her community when the Taliban took control of the area in 2009. The extremists banned many things, like owning a television and playing music. They enforced harsh punishments for those who defied their orders. And, alarmingly, they said girls could no longer go to school. This never happens to boys.

Malala started writing about her dissatisfaction and even created blogs under a false name for BBC Urdu – a service transmitting to millions across Asia. In 2011, Archbishop Desmond Tutu nominated Malala for the International Children's Peace Prize. That same year, she met with the Prime Minister of Pakistan who awarded her the country's National Peace Award for Youth, in recognition of her bravery. All this notoriety added risks for Malala. Being famous and female wasn't to the Taliban's liking.

In October 2012, on her way home from school, a masked Taliban gunman boarded her bus, asked *'Who is Malala?'* and, when she stood up defiantly, shot her in the head.

She woke up 10 days later in Queen Elizabeth Hospital in Birmingham, England. The doctors and nurses told her about the attack and that people around the world were praying for her recovery. After months of surgeries and rehabilitation, she was able to join her family in their new home in England. It was then she knew she had a choice: she could live a quiet and normal life, just like her new-found school friends, or she could make the most of this new life whilst also using her shocking experience (seen by the whole world) as a platform to speak up and to initiate change. She was determined to continue her fight until every girl could go to school as a right, not a privilege.

She started the Malala Fund, investing in education for girls wherever finances are not forthcoming. She also started a series of speeches all around the world about the inalienable right of all humans to an education. In 2014, she became the youngest recipient of the Nobel Peace Prize.

For me, Malala is more than a Captain of positive change. She is a beacon of hope, a symbol of bravery against all odds. She is a living martyr.

Fake news: Women cannot compete with men.

Billie Jean King

I was one of the fascinated spectators for the most-watched tennis match of all time. Remarkably, it was more than 50 years ago (1973) that Billie Jean King challenged and beat a leading male player who had been a Grand Slam champion himself. Bobby Riggs had been outspoken in his view that women could not compete with men in a straight physical challenge, epitomised by a game of tennis. Over 90 million people watched Billie Jean beat Bobby Riggs in three competitive sets and create an iconic, cultural moment symbolising women's equality.

As I grew up in Wimbledon and played in the junior competition at the Championships, Billie Jean was already a legend for me as an athlete. She was a phenomenal, fearsome talent, winning an astonishing 36 Grand Slam titles. What marked her out as a player for me was that despite not being the tallest, fastest or strongest player, she was easily the smartest and fiercest at that time. She possesses a potent intellectual and attitudinal combination which she brings to all aspects of her resolute activism.

What marks her out even more than her athletic achievements is that she is a symbol of courage, equality and leadership. She has used the platform that talent gave her to change the world for women and for the LBGT community. Her mark on mankind is indelible. (I note the irony in using a masculine word like mankind to describe everybody.)

Here are just a few headlines of Billie Jean's focus and impact:

- She champions equality and inclusion in the workplace.
- She was the lead spokesperson for the Title IX law that prohibits sex-based discrimination in federally funded education and athletics – the inspiration for Missy Park's clothing business!

- She founded the WTA (Women's Tennis Association) to promote fair treatment and an equal voice in decision-making across the sport (astonishingly, the first equal pay tournament was as early as the US Open in 1973).

- She promoted and achieved equal pay for professional female tennis players, engrained in law.

- She was one of the first prominent athletes to be openly gay, removing what was, and still can be, a life-defining stigma for many.

Queen Elizabeth II: My Number ONE Captain

When Queen Elizabeth II died in September 2022, I was sitting in my car in a multi-storey car park in Manchester. I cried. In fact, I sobbed audibly. I was truly surprised at this emotional reaction until I reflected on why I felt so overcome with sadness. Elizabeth was the only monarch I had known for my entire life; all sixty years. Her crest is on our post boxes, her face is on all the stamps we use. I felt loss even though her declining health had meant the end had been imminent and inevitable. I had cried because the leader I most admire for being a role model of sustained positive impact, humility and selfless service would no longer be a constant in my life. For Captaincy here, read constancy.

Her famous promise to her multigenerational peoples at the tender age of 21 was fulfilled for 70 transformational years:

> *'My whole life, whether it be long or short, shall be devoted to your service.'*

As the Head of the Commonwealth in 1952, Elizabeth presided as a figure head over eight countries. When she died, 48 more countries had willingly joined the coalition, representing 2.5 billion people. Much of that growth in fealty (sworn loyalty to a Lord) stems from Queen Elizabeth's character, humanised communication and remarkable work ethic. She generated a spirit of multicultural togetherness and trust.

Queen Elizabeth demonstrated for seven decades how to lead with personal character and strategic and verbal restraint. In a world full of bluster, noise and exaggeration, she led with simple, symbolic authority. The best example of her restraint combined with explicit signalling is when the United Kingdom voted to leave the European Union in 2016. The Queen never said a word about her views on the decision, either before it was made, during the campaign, or indeed after the decision had been ratified. However, her outfit and demeanour at the first public event after the UK's decision sent a clear message to her European allies, *'This was not my call and I am not amused.'*

I have a profound sense of history. I studied the subject at university and specialised in European colonisation of Africa, 1880–1900. My mother, Beate Ohlhagen, lived through The Blitz in Hamburg throughout the summer of 1943, and my father, Richard Francis, was knighted by the Queen for services to the BBC and the British Council. He was lauded for his diplomacy and contribution as the Controller of BBC Northern Ireland during The Troubles.

If you would like to know more about my dad, who was very much a Captain of free speech in the media, please seek out *The BBC's Last Warrior Statesman* written by my eldest brother, Stephen Francis.

It is not lost on me as a historian that the British Empire created lasting trauma for many. It's not lost on me that Queen Elizabeth resided over the final years of the British Empire under the sobriquet of a 'Commonwealth'. And it's not lost on me that for many, she was a symbol of British tyranny.

Elizabeth's state visit to the Republic of Ireland in 2011 was the first by a British monarch since its independence. Her speech at Dublin Castle, where she expressed deep sympathy for the suffering caused by Britain's past actions, was a moving and powerful gesture of reconciliation. It helped tangibly to ease long-standing tensions across the island of Ireland.

On that occasion, she also made a seminal visit to the Garden of Remembrance in Dublin, which honours those who fought for Irish independence. This included those who had been involved in the murder of her cousin and close friend, Louis Mountbatten, in 1979.

As the monarch of 16 different independent countries, Queen Elizabeth did not set governmental policy in any of them, but her countless symbolic actions, courteous demeanour and carefully crafted words made her a unique figure in fostering diplomacy, reconciliation and goodwill between nations.

At the state banquet in Dublin on 18th May 2011, she affirmed, *'Whatever life throws at us, our individual responses will be all the stronger for working together and sharing the load.'*

In 1986, her visit to meet Deng Xiaoping was the first by any British monarch to China. Her non-partisan, ceremonial diplomacy showed deep respect for Asian culture. It helped smooth relationships between two countries with a complex colonial history. She had paved the way for the government of Hong Kong to be returned to the Chinese state in 1997.

The enormity of her impact is reflected in how she made people feel and respond. Early in her reign in the late 1950s, she embarked on a state visit to the US. She elected to arrive in Chicago by boat from across Lake Michigan. In response, the city built a special pier in her honour, and more than one million Chicagoans lined the lakeshore to greet her. By comparison, that number is four times more people than the fervent, spell-bound crowds who attended change-maker President Obama's acceptance speech in Chicago, his hometown, in November 2008!

In her Christmas address to the nation in 2014, she reaffirmed her core intent to be a healer:

> *'Sometimes it seems that reconciliation stands little chance in the face of war and discord. But as the Christmas truce a century ago reminds us, peace and goodwill have lasting power in the hearts of men and women.'*

The Final Tip
Em Stroud

Even clowns can be Captains. The final tip I'll share comes to you from a real-life clown called Em Stroud. Em makes me laugh, she makes me think positive thoughts and she inspires me to play. Here's the first words of her TED Talk to establish and reinforce this intentionality:

> 'I want the future for all of us to be filled with laughing. I want the future to be filled with thinking; thinking kind thoughts about ourselves and kind thoughts about other people. I want the future for all of us to be filled with play. When we laugh, think and play, we connect. When we connect, we can change the world.'

Em's presentation as a guest speaker at a Uspire Leaders' Paradigm Shifter conference in 2023 inspired me to prepare for all my meetings and interactions with a clear and written-down intention. I aim to be intentional as a grandparent too. Every time I see my eighteen-month-old granddaughter Lavinia Jay, my intention is to communicate at eye level and laugh with her a lot. In fact, we mainly mimic each other and giggle at the simplest of things! Have a read of Em's book *Lessons From a Clown* – it's simple and an inspiring message.

After my determination to be intentional every day had become engrained for me, fate brought me to a meeting with a new colleague based in Germany, Markus

Lemme. Markus is a training champion who taught me a great tool called T.I.P. It helps to crystalise Em's concept of intentionality. With my high yellow energy, it usually takes me two minutes to write my T.I.P. before a business meeting. I commend it for you to use now to either sharpen your thinking about something you already Captain, or indeed to shape a new intention to be a Captain of a much-needed change.

Here is how T.I.P. works:

<u>T</u> is for your targets (plural).

1. What is your emotional target for the interaction/meeting? How do you want to feel in this interaction? What emotions do you want to engender in the other person/people? Do you want them to feel surprise, excitement and commitment? Do you want them to feel saddened about an event or topic and thereby determined to act?

2. The second target should be specific, logical and numerical. What needs to be accomplished and by what specific date? For example, '*1,000 signed-up members and 5 million followers on social media by the end of next year.*'

3. The third target is about process. What are the steps you need to take over the medium to long-term (and in sequence) to achieve your dream big goal and related numerical targets? For example: 1. *Find five allies* 2. *Set milestones together* 3. *Get funding* 4. *Social media launch.*

I is for the information that you already have that needs to be shared with the others you are about to interact with. It is also about listing the key information you still need to gather or learn in the interaction. For example: *'Share my goal and initial plan.'* Learn from their opinions, other options and related financial imperatives. What might hold them back from signing up to this adventure?

P stands for your plan for the specific communication or meeting. For example: *1. Start with a fun, related story hook. 2. Facilitate a discussion about everyone's opinions and personal aspirations 3. Set a short-term shared intention 4. Set a date for the next meeting.*

As a Captain of Change, use T.I.P. to prepare your journey and enrol your tribe.

Remind yourself of all the skills and behaviours to dial up on your Captain's journey. The Champion stories in this book bring these traits to life for you, so start by choosing which are already your superpowers. Focus first and mainly on those. As for the others, use it as a checklist of improvement and/or recruit new tribe members who bring what you are missing!

The Bottom Line

1. Choose what you want to Captain **with passion**
2. Get started
3. Don't stop until you succeed

Reflect on who captured your attention the most in this chapter and look to replicate their attitude, focus and relentless energy. What did they do that's your biggest *Oh!* and crucially, what's the overriding *And So?* in terms of action?

OH	SO

Conclusion

Everyone can be a Captain. You just need to step up, step in and step on it!

O Captain! My Captain!'

Rise up and hear the bells;
Rise up – for you the flag is flung – for you the bugle trills,
For you the bouquets and ribbon'd wreaths –
For you the shores a-crowding,
For you they call, the swaying mass, their eager faces turning;
Here Captain!

This is an extract from Walt Whitman's famous poem that was written in reverence to Captain Abraham Lincoln's journey from the Illinois militia (1832) to US President (1861).

Go through the notes you have made from reading this book and pick up the main themes that resonated for you. If needs be, find the person who inspires you the most in *The Captaincy* and take inspiration from them to act. You have 60 Champion stories to choose from! What related intentions do you have?

Pick a cause both important for you and worth fighting for. Write out a big, bold Captain's goal for it, and take the first step soon.

Envision the outcomes intended from your Captaincy, and bring colour and emotion to that imagery. How will success in the endeavour make you feel? What impact will it have on others? See it, hear it, feel it.

Above all, if you have always stopped yourself from stepping up, take a big, deep breath (or a few!), gird yourself and make the leap.

References and Further Reading

Chapter 1

Malcolm Gladwell, *Blink: The Power of Thinking Without Thinking*, Penguin, 2006

Mihaly Csikszentmihalyi, *Flow: The Psychology of Optimal Experience*, Harper Perennial, 2008

David Epstein, *The Sports Gene: Talent, Practice and the Truth About Success*, Yellow Jersey, 2014

Gavin Hastings, *Legacy of the Lions: Lessons in Leadership from the British & Irish Lions*, Polaris Publishing Ltd, 2021

Arianna Huffington, *On becoming fearless... in love, work and life*, Little, Brown, 2007

Serena Williams (with Daniel Paisner), *My Life, Queen of the Court*, Simon & Schuster Ltd, 2009

Chapter 2

Women and Peace and Security Report of the Secretary-General, United Nation Security Council, S/2021/827, September 2021, https://www.securitycouncilreport.org/atf/cf/%7B65BFCF9B-6D27-4E9C-8CD3-CF6E4FF96FF9%7D/s_2021_827.pdf

Jacinda Ardern, *A Different Kind of Power*, Macmillan, 2025

Thomas Erikson, *Surrounded by Idiots: The Four Types of Human Behaviour (or, How to Understand Those Who Cannot Be Understood)*, Vermilion, 2019

Mike Brearley, *The Art of Captaincy*, Hodder & Stoughton, 1985

Noelle Ingram, *She's the Boss: 9 Powerful Steps To Mastering Leadership For New Female Leaders In Business*, independently published, 2023

Podcast: Adam Grant, Re:Thinking, www.adamgrant.net/podcasts/rethinking

Title Nine, www.titlenine.com/t9-pitchfest

Chapter 3

Martyn Thomas, *World in Their Hands: The Story of the First Women's Rugby World Cup*, Polaris Publishing Ltd, 2022

Blaire Palmer, *Punks in Suits: How to lead the workplace reformation*, Rethink Press, 2024

Chapter 4

Ali Stewart and Derek Biddle, *The Pioneer: A powerful blueprint for greater success in your life and career*, Rethink Press, 2024

Ali Stewart and Derek Biddle, *Liberating Leadership: Leading and Developing High-Performance*, Rethink Press, 2015

Sam Walker, *The Captain Class: The Hidden Forces Behind The World's Greatest Teams*, Ebury Press, 2017

Beringer Vineyards: www.beringer.com

Three Sources suggesting 90% of our decisions are negative: Antonio Damasio's research (1994)

Gerald Zaltman, *How Customers Think*, Harvard Business Press, 2003

Daniel Kahneman, *Thinking, Fast and Slow*, Penguin, 2012

Chapter 5

Taibi Kahler, *The Mastery of Management: Or How to Solve the Mystery of Mismanagement*, Kahler Communications, 1992

Carl Jung, *Collected Works, Vol 11, Psychology and Religion West and East* (translated from the German by R.F.C. Hull), Routledge, 1970

Baz Moffat, *The Female Body Bible*, Bantam, 2024

Sun Tzu, *The Art of War* (translated from the Chinese by Jonathan Clements), Macmillan Collectors Library, 2017

Chin Ning Chu, *Thick Face, Black Heart: the Warrior Philosophy for Conquering the Challenges of Business and Life*, Balance, 1994

Song: Queen, *Fat Bottomed Girls*, lyrics and music by Brian May, 1978

Chapter 6

Nick Francis, *The New Fire*, Compass Publishing UK, 2019

Chapter 7

Anthony Willoughby Territory Mapping, https://territorymapping.pro

Aduke Onofowokan, *The Act of Inclusion*, Horizon Collective, www.horizoncollective.org

Bep Dhaliwal, Thrive365, www.thrive365.co.uk

Chapter 8

Raymond Meredith Belbin, *Management Teams: Why They Succeed or Fail*, Routledge, 2010

Chapter 9

Pam Warren, *From Behind the Mask*, Biteback, 2014

Mike Adams, *Seven Stories Every Salesperson Must Tell*, Michael Hanrahan Publishing, 2018

Song: Johnny Preston, *Running Bear*, music and lyrics by J.P. Richardson, 1959

Chapter 10

James Kerr, *Legacy: What the All Blacks Can Teach Us About the Business of Life*, Constable, 2013

Abby Wambach, *Wolfpack: How to Come Together, Unleash Our Power and Change the Game*, Piatkus, 2019

Chapter 11

Stephen Francis, *The BBC's Last Warrior Statesman*, independently published, 2025

Em Stroud, *Lessons From a Clown: How To Find Courage To Show Up For Yourself and Laugh Every Day*, Nielsen Book Services, 2021

Conclusion

Poem: Walt Whitman, 'O *Captain! My Captain!*', The Saturday Press, 1865

Glossary of Leadership Models

Model	Descriptor	Originator
SpQ	4 elements of sporting intelligence	Mark Francis, 2024
Cognitive Reframing	Change what you think about something important	Aaron T. Beck, Cognitive Therapy, 1968
T.E.A.R.	4 steps to assist cognitive reframing: Thoughts Emotions Actions Results	Kevin Walsh, 2018, Miami Beach, Florida
Colour Energies	4 core personality styles	Carl Jung / Colour Insights
A.B.C.D.	Think audience/ behaviour before content and delivery	Forbes Communication Council ABCDE (2023)

Hooks	4 best ways to get full attention at the meeting's start	Aristotle, Demosthenes & Isocrates 5th–4th century BC
Logical Levels Pyramid	Different levels of people's experience, influencing behaviours	Robert Dilts, NLP, 1982
Backward Planning	Start planning backwards in steps from the final outcome	Stephen Covey, *The 7 Habits of the Highly Successful*, 1989
Milestone Planning	Breaking down large projects into phases with end date sequential steps	Project Management 101
VMDE	4 steps for liberating leaders	Ali Stewart and Derek Biddle, 2016
8 leader competencies	The two main competencies for each of the VMDE phases of leadership	Mark Francis, Kate Greaves & Philip J H Crocker, 2016
5 Drivers	5 common drivers that motivate us	Taibi Kahler, 1975
Personal Brand Key	Mark's adapted key for personal brand	Robert Passikoff, 1984

AI Territory Mapping	A way of gaining clarity/purpose by mapping what you hunt, protect/grow	Anthony Willoughby, 1966 AI: Francisco Aceituna 2025
High-Gain Questions	Targeted open-ended questions	Multiple sources
Stakeholder Maps	Plotting all interested parties connected to a specific decision	Aubrey L. Mendelow, 1991
T.I.P.	Helps you plan any meeting with targets, information needed and the plan	Markus Lemme, Factor 4, 2022

About the Author

When I was called to the Headmaster's office while approaching my final year at school, I assumed it was for a pep talk about too much sport and not enough academic endeavour. Robin Reeve, as the newly arrived Headmaster of King's College School in Wimbledon, had other ideas:

'I need to choose my first Captain of School. I'd like that to be you, Mark. I see how you influence those around you, both on the sports field and off it.' I asked the new headteacher for a day to consider the offer. I was heavily dyslexic and innately shy, so just the thought of speaking in public made me anxious, distracted and visibly insecure. Nevertheless, my mum gave me the courage to say yes and in September 1981, a reluctant Captain was born.

At Lancaster University (1982–1986), I was Athletic Union President for a year and began to believe I might quite like taking charge in a business capacity too. My career moved from commercial leadership in fast-moving consumer goods, in two businesses based in England (Whitbread Beer Company and United Biscuits), to a global role centred in Geneva. My last corporate job was as the Vice President of Global Human Resources (HR) for a Japanese organisation (JTI), where I oversaw 14,000 staff and could seamlessly fake being a cerebral global leader, with no HR background at all.

In all my leadership roles, I proved to be a better coach than manager. In 2002, I took the plunge and set up my own business in consultancy. Augmenta Ltd, originally based in Switzerland, is dedicated to commercial training and development coaching. My core purpose is to grow confidence and skill in leaders so they transform their people capability and related business outcomes.

By happenstance, my first clients were big, multinational organisations (Danone and Edwards Lifesciences) and it meant I continued to travel to all corners of the world, expanding my experience of how leaders impact their teams. It's a thrill to say those first two clients remain significant partners on my journey today, nearly a quarter of a century later.

Throughout, I combined a full work schedule with playing and coaching multiple sports. I have been an active coach of women's rugby since 1982 and was at Richmond Rugby Club in a coaching capacity for 30 years.

I met Debbie there and we married in 1989. We have three boys who are all as sporty as their parents: Ben (33), James (29) and Tom (23).

About the Author

On top of the Breya Mountain, Valais in Switzerland: Mark, Ben, Debbie, Tom and James.

You can find me on:

LinkedIn: search for Mark (Peter Charles) Francis

Instagram: @markpetercharles

mark@theuspirepartnership.com

www.augmenta.co.uk
(for insight into influencing different nationalities)

www.theuspirepartnership.com

The Role Model Effect

Right from birth, we are wired for imitation. We mimic accents, habits, even ambitions – especially when we see someone 'like us' succeed. That's the role model effect in action:

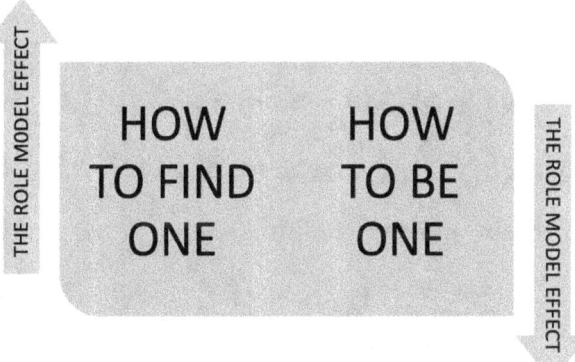

Most Captains have used a person they know (or know of) as a model of what they themselves would like to be. In your quest to be a role model, set behavioural standards yourself – that could be as simple as no phone use after 6pm or before 9am.

THE ROLE MODEL EFFECT

 FIND ONE

Pick someone who is breaking new ground.

Pick people whose values match yours.

Pick without age as a criteria… younger than you could be better.

 **BE ONE**

Tell people you are open to playing a role.

Tell them your greatest wins and biggest lessons.

Lift them up as they climb.

One act of courage can start a chain reaction; be the reason someone else believes.

If you found value in this book, please write a review on Amazon, Waterstones and Goodreads.

www.ingramcontent.com/pod-product-compliance
Lightning Source LLC
Chambersburg PA
CBHW071155070526
44584CB00019B/2804